A Cup of Honey

The story of a young Holocaust survivor,
Eliezer Ayalon

by Neile Sue Friedman

SelectBooks, Inc.
New York

This edition published by SelectBooks, Inc.
For information address SelectBooks, Inc., New York, New York.

First Edition

ISBN 978-1-59079-365-7

Manufactured in the United States of America
10 9 8 7 6 5 4 3 2 1

Dedication

We dedicate this book to the blessed memory of Eli's family, who perished in the Holocaust:

Eli's parents, Rivka Leah and Israel Hershenfis; his brothers, Mayer Munish and Abush Wolf Hershenfis; and his sister, Chaya Branka Hershenfis.

We also dedicate this book to both of our families, in the United States and Israel, whose support has been invaluable:

Anna Friedman, Lily Friedman, Joseph Friedman and John Friedman; and Neile's husband, Steve Eisner, author and owner of When Words Count Writers' Retreat in Rochester, Vermont, who inspired us to republish the book two decades after it was first published in order to keep the story alive; and

Rivka Ayalon, Ofer and Hannah Ayalon, Nurit and Yaacov Atar, Gil and Keren Ayalon, Yifat Ayalon Elkayam, Neta and Yoni Mor, Omri Atar, Almog Atar, Yuval and Liam Elkayam, Mia Ayalon and Noa and Nadav Mor.

In our children, grandchildren and great-grandchildren we see the bright future of the Jewish people, linked to memories of the past.

About the Author

NEILE SUE FRIEDMAN'S legal career has spanned nearly three decades. As an administrative law judge for the State of Maryland for almost twenty years, Neile hears and decides cases for dozens of state government agencies that have a meaningful daily impact on people's lives. Her experience writing *A Cup of Honey* reminds her every day of the consequences to individuals when governments improperly restrict civil rights. This perspective guides Neile's work, and helps to ensure that agency decisions are just.

Previously Neile worked for ten years as an assistant attorney general, serving as counsel to the State of Maryland in its efforts to develop and implement water pollution prevention programs to clean up the Chesapeake Bay, and as prosecutor of violators of our clean air and water acts and laws for disposal of hazardous waste.

Neile, who has three grown children, Anna, Lily, and Joseph, lives in Baltimore. She is married to Steve Eisner, who runs a writers' retreat in Rochester, Vermont.

Acknowledgements

We would like to acknowledge the following family members, friends, colleagues and organizations, both in Israel and in the United States, without whose help and encouragment this project would not have been realized: Dr. Eyal Bor; Judge Aaron Cohn; Michael Drukman; Lynn Flaisher; Vena Gibbs; E. Scott Johnson; Scott A. Johnson; Diane Kempler; Jill Kneerim; Yocheved Henriques Koplowitz; Elanore Lampner; Elizabeth Landon; Lyndsey Layton; Pola Mandelbaum; Jerry Molen; Marcia Moylan; Shamai Perlman; Jezyk Rosenberg; Marcy Silver; Jacqueline and Robert Smelkinson; Anne Marie Stein; Marc B. Terrill; David and Carolyn Thaler; Beverly Wolpert; Moshe Yanover; Yad Vashem Archives, Jerusalem; The Central Zionist Archives, Jerusalem; The Youth Immigration Department of the Jewish Agency for Israel; The United Jewish Appeal; The Radom House; THE ASSOCIATED: Jewish Community Federation of Baltimore; The Jewish Federation of Greater Dallas; The Combined Jewish Philanthropies of Boston; The Los Angeles Jewish Federation.

Neile Sue Friedman and Eliezer Ayalon

Preface

A sealed room in Jerusalem. January, 1991. I am no longer a child — I have children myself — even grandchildren. The War ended many years ago.

My childhood years were trapped inside sealed places. Closed off streets. A walled ghetto. Sealed borders. Bolted boxcars. Barracks, locked. Camps guarded with machine guns. Barbed wire fencing, electrified.

A gas chamber. Sealed tight. Very dirty. Cold. Dark. Yelling outside. Loud wailing inside. Mothers clinging to their small children, trying to soothe them. Not to worry, my little one. Mama is holding Chaya, protecting her. Tears fall effortlessly from desperate eyes. Bodies tremble uncontrollably in fright. In my imagination they cling to each other until the end.

Has my home in Jerusalem become a gas chamber? Impossible. We have an army. A government. The world would not let a madman suffocate us with gas fumes. It happened already, a long time ago, and the world learned a lesson. "Never again," we said.

I watch the healthy, confident face of my small grandson. It is 2:00 in the morning, and he is sitting in a corner of the sealed room, with his gas mask on. He plays happily with a fire engine, making siren noises. It is hard to hear him. The mask makes him sound like he is in a barrel. Trapped in the barrel. He is not afraid. He feels lucky to be up late. The real siren — the air raid siren —is loud. It rings in my ears. I cover my ears to make the sound go away.

My mother would hold me in her arms. She would whisper to me. "With God's will," she would say, "everything will be all right." I want to see Mama's face. Her smile. Her comforting eyes.

Gas masks. We each have been provided with one. My family look like insects in them. Like insects caught in a trap. Flies. Gigantic ones. In a few moments the air will run out. The gas will fill the room like a big yellow cloud. Each breath will make us dizzy. We will panic. Our faces will contort. We will try to breathe, but no air will enter our lungs. We will begin to climb the walls. To try to escape. We can't escape — the room is sealed.

This is not rational, of course. Our government has prepared us well for this nightmare. The room is sealed with a special plastic to keep the gas out. Door openings are sealed with wet rags and thick tape. This is the opposite of a gas chamber. The gas masks will protect us from the harmful effects of any gas that might sneak inside from the Jerusalem hills. We enjoy all the modern defenses against gas attacks. We have a television — cable television. A radio. Up-to-the-minute news bulletins. Bottles of pure mineral water. This is 1991. I am in Jerusalem. We are perfectly safe inside this sealed room — it shelters our pale faces and trembling bodies.

I refuse to put on my gas mask. My wife is angry with me. So is my pregnant daughter. They cannot persuade me to do it. Not that it would be uncomfortable. The experts made sure the fit was perfect. Not that I would not know how to use it. We have been trained well, and have practiced. We even joked about it. People wear gas masks to clean up chemical spills. We have seen that in the evenings on CNN.

My wife and daughter cannot understand why I refuse to put it on. They tell me I am stubborn. I think I am invincible, they say.

I do not hear them anymore. I cannot see them either. Their faces have become a blur. They shake me, but I do not feel anything. I want to be with Mama and Chaya. Mama would hold us tightly together. "You will have a sweet life, my darling." I want to suffer like they did. The gas must take me to them. I do not deserve this life — joys, happiness, comfort, pleasure. Grandchildren. A beautiful home in a golden city. I breathe deeply, wishing to be carried away. Then, blackness...

Kinderyoren [Childhood Years]

Eli's translation of old Yiddish children's ballad.

Childhood, dear and sweet childhood.
You remain in my memory forever.
When I think about your years, they seem to me
    everlasting.
Like a dream you vanished.

I can see my home in front of my eyes.
Where I was born and raised.
I can see my cradle there
Which still stands in the same spot.
Like a dream you vanished.

And my mama whom I used to love,
Even though she chased me to the religious school
Every pinch from her hand
Is so well known to me.
But no signs are left behind.

And I can see you, Ruchele, my dear one,
How I kiss your red cheeks.
Your eyes, full of charm,
Penetrate my heart.
I thought you would remain mine.

Childhood, I have lost you.
And my dear mama, I have lost you too.
Childhood, very sad, dark, and bitter.
Like a dream you vanished.

Introduction

A Cup of Honey: The Story of a Young Holocaust Survivor, Eliezer Ayalon was originally published in English in 1999; Hebrew and Spanish translations followed. Although Eli had been a veteran tour guide for special educational/cultural journeys, called "missions," to Israel organized by the Jewish Federations of North America, he had not disclosed his astonishing personal story to the public, even to people who joined his mission groups.

Although Eli was often animated and brimming with stories, he also had revealed little of his experience during the war to his own family. While survivor guilt and shame were partly to blame for this, Eli, like many others, felt that people would not believe his story because it was so horrific. Also, at the time of Israel's early nation building, the top priority was the need for the tiny new country to respond effectively to existential threats and multiple wars. In those years Israelis were necessarily looking forward, and many survivors, like Eli, changed their pre-war names, learned and adopted their new language of Hebrew and silently swept away the untold, and to most, inexplicable events of the past.

When I first met Eli on a mission to Israel in December 1991, I could sense he harbored secrets. The day our group arrived, we traveled with him as our guide to the newly opened Atlit Museum, near Haifa on the Mediterranean coast. When we arrived at this destination, Eli oddly walked off by himself, and we did not see him again until we boarded the bus for our next stop.

Others guided us through the exhibits that depict a tragic and bizarre chapter in Word War II and Jewish history. Many Jewish refugees, who had successfully escaped Nazi persecution, sailed to British-controlled Palestine only to find themselves imprisoned in Atlit detention camp, similar in appearance and form to Nazi concentration camps. From the time the war ended in May of 1945 until 1948, estimates of tens of thousands of "illegal" Jewish immigrants were detained there by the British as part of their policy of severely limiting Jewish immigration to Palestine.

In 1945 there was a shocking incident where orphaned Jewish refugee children who had been rescued by the Jewish Brigade, and granted special permission to enter Palestine legally, were required by the British Mandatory Authority to be housed at Atlit detention camp— albeit temporarily, for "disinfection."

When Eli disappeared before our museum tour, I suspected there was a story he was not telling. Later my group woke up at 2:00 a.m. for an hour bus trip to the airport to greet a planeload of newly arriving immigrants from the former Soviet Union. I invited Eli to sit with me.

"Why did you go off when we arrived at Atlit, Eli?" I asked him. "I didn't," he insisted and added, "I just went to get a coffee." I didn't buy his explanation. "Come on Eli, you were gone for over an hour. What happened?"

And Eli's story started to emerge—just like that while everyone slept except the two of us. Eli sat in the window seat of the bus, hands stuffed protectively into the pockets of his light gray bomber jacket. "I was a prisoner there," he whispered, "and it hurts to see the place reconstructed. I cannot do it."

I felt goose bumps. Eli's emotions, even his words, were raw and unfiltered; his face downcast. He was describing experiences and feelings from long ago to another for the very first time:

It was just after the War that I arrived there. I remember that day well. When I close my eyes, I see everything in front of me. When we entered the camp, we immediately saw fierce looking armed soldiers on the ground and even in watchtowers; the camp was surrounded by barbed wire, so we were trapped . . . caged. They forced us to separate from the girls, to undress and then to enter large shower rooms; they even sprayed us with DDT. We were children, and so we began crying, screaming. I was scared and confused. I felt humiliated—like I was back in Europe with the Nazis.

That's why I went away, Neile. I wanted to walk a little, to gather myself. Dahhling, there are some things even you cannot possibly understand. At the museum, they recreated the disinfection room. I cannot walk inside because it takes me back. I do not want to go back.

And so I heard how it happened that in that November of 1945, after disembarking the Princess Kathleen ship that had transported Eli and the other children out of Europe, Eli entered Atlit where he and the children were astonished once again to be greeted with the horrors of barbed wire, manned guard towers, disinfection chambers, separation of boys from girls, cold wooden barracks, and roll calls.

But Eli also went back, way back. He talked and talked. In these early days of our writing collaboration, I heard just snippets—about broken legs, abscessed skin, ghettos, work details, mine explosions, a little about his mother. The snippets were enough to suck me in. I wanted to know more, and Eli wanted to tell me more. Others on the bus later admitted that they overheard portions of our conversation and were jealous that Eli was talking to me alone.

But how could he tell me more? I lived an ocean away. And why? After all these years, why was he telling me these stories, and why did I want to hear them? Well, the "how" we worked out. He would come to Baltimore, and I would travel to Jerusalem. We would also travel around the United States, and in Europe to visit archives, museums, and libraries holding important materials documenting the day-to-day life in the places figuring prominently in the book. We wanted to accurately reflect the names, places, and dates of his events. We would also visit or telephone individuals whose lives Eli touched along the way to cross-check their memories against Eli's.

For Eli, it was time to open up after all those years. When he met Eli Wiesel, Mr. Wiesel had instructed Eli that as a survivor it was his duty to tell his story. Eli's mother had imparted a similar message: that it was "meant to be" that Eli must survive the War in order to tell his story and keep the memory of his family alive. For Eli, the time had come because his children and grandchildren needed to know about their family.

And for me, the more I heard about Eli's experience, the more I wanted to hear. As a mother of small children, I related to the boy whose story Eli was telling. I connected emotionally to his mother, too, especially after I saw her photograph, with those large and beautiful dark, proud eyes that appeared to look directly into mine, imploring me to help Eli. I was in awe how a mother, facing extraordinary circumstances, could muster the strength to urge her smallest child to set out alone into the uncertain world of German-occupied Poland while the rest of the family at least faced their uncertainty together. It was important for me to help accomplish her final wish for Eli: that he survive in order to tell the story of his family. And, of course, I wanted my children to hear the tale; I was certain they would benefit from seeing their mother in the process of uncovering it.

During the mission that December, Eli and I spent more and more time together discussing his childhood. After the mission returned to the United States, I stayed in Israel for an extra week, completely taken by Eli's stories as we continued our sessions. After a while, we, along with our families, decided to pursue the project: I would write Eli's biography.

* * *

WHILE SLOW, THE PROCESS OF uncovering Eli's repressed memories was yielding valuable information and insights. I would interview Eli until I felt I was living in the moment; then I would write his story. Finally we would take what I had written and fill in detail as well as dialogue. We cross-checked the facts and this process triggered even more memories. Eli recalled songs from his childhood, and as he sang them, additional anecdotes were revealed.

This process kept expanding and Eli's life-story started taking shape. I was happy because I felt I was opening up treasured memories and that this was important work. And so, for the next five or six years we carried on in this way, using old-fashioned PC computers with floppy discs and dot matrix printers. It was a life-changing collaboration for both Eli and me. I will never forget the day when we finished a first draft of the book. It was in 1993. The book would end up being changed significantly, with many stories added, but finally we had a beginning, middle, and end. We selected a title, calling it "Beshert," or "Meant to Be." My husband took the pages to a copier store and created bound copies. When Eli opened the box of the bound copies and saw his story in print, he started to cry. He felt that his life was finally validated. He was proud. He would never again feel the need to conceal his history.

And the publication of the book in 1999 changed Eli dramatically. Becoming a powerful, articulate, and charismatic public speaker, he suddenly felt liberated from his self-imposed silence, and found his calling. He began to speak to his tour participants about his experiences as a teenager in the Holocaust. He also started to lead international groups through the Holocaust History Museum at Yad Vashem as part of educational seminars and workshops, and as a lecturer with the Yad Vashem International School for Holocaust Studies. This led to invitations from around the world for Eli to share, in person, his powerful personal story.

Eli traveled throughout the United States visiting places that included Michigan, Arizona, Maryland, New York, New Jersey, Massachusetts, Florida, Texas, California, and Oklahoma, as well as Mexico, Costa Rica, and Europe. He lectured at conferences, schools, universities, and community centers.

As a witness to the events of the Holocaust, he led dozens of delegations to concentration camps and former Jewish communities in Poland. Relating to groups of all kinds was Eli's gift. He was well received by Jewish and non-Jewish groups from many continents, including American Amish groups who eschewed their traditional restrictions on using modern technology by boarding planes and busses to visit the holy land. He related equally well to children and adults, men and women.

In 1998 he addressed a group of Native American tribal elders who were moved by their deep feelings about the similarities between their story and Eli's. As Oklahoma City's News9 recounted at the time, Shoshana Wasserman, public relations officer for the American Indian Cultural Center and Museum explained, "The process of moving to Israel and beginning a new life and defeating Hitler, by the very fact that he has started a family and a legacy. . . I think our native people feel very much the same way, that we were meant to be extinct, and yet, we're here, we're resilient."

Speaking about the Holocaust became an obsession for Eli. He saw it as critical because the generation of Holocaust survivor witnesses was getting older. As Eli explained in 2011:

> In 10-15 years, there will be no survivors that can utter the simple words: 'I was there and I experienced this.' The world must remember the extermination camps, not because we seek to arouse pity and compassion for ourselves—it is too late for that—the world needs to know about hunger and starvation today and about those who perished, to denounce the insanity

of genocide and the ugliness of war and the banality of evil. You must speak out against prejudice, bigotry, racism, baseless hatred, because silence can kill— through the Holocaust we have seen how silence can kill millions."

And Eli was very good at telling his life story. As Natalie Page from Yad Vashem explained when Eli spoke to a crowd there about his experiences, especially about the life-changing moment when he was separated from his mother, Eli's "impact on audiences would be visible." Crowds were mesmerized by Eli's intensely personal and animated storytelling. When Eli narrated an event happening in a place long ago and far away, he brought you to that place and time. He made you feel what he felt; he painted scenes, acted out voices, and even sang songs that would vividly bring moments to life in your head. He used his hands, eyes, and facial expressions for emphasis. You would laugh and cry with him; it was so very powerfully intimate.

When he spoke with children, he would sing lullabies his mother used to sing to him to illustrate his loving home; he would talk about playing soccer with his friends in the street, watching cowboy movies at the Kino Apollo and sleeping on a straw mattress in a warm and comfortable one-room house, and then he would gently discuss how the Nazis took everything away from him simply because he was Jewish.

With adults, Eli was more graphic. As Allyson Rockwell captured on film in her documentary, *Eli,*

Inspiring Future Generations, Eli would transport the listener into the past. Speaking at the site of the former Plaszow Concentration Camp, where Eli, while recuperating from a near-deadly left leg abscess in the sick-house, was forced to witness daily executions of women, children, older people, even whole families "like birds at a shooting range," Eli described the experience to a group:

> [*After pausing to collect himself.*] I needed a few moments to myself in order to bring me back to this place. When I'm standing here on the hill . . . I show you an open graveyard, a mass grave, like a crater. And if I will take you down to [the bottom] I will ask you to pick up some of the soil and you can feel little pieces of bones and ashes in your fingers. So, you don't see anything here! People don't see anything. But when I close my eyes for a minute or two minutes, and I look around, I can see the layout of the camp! Everything. . . . Lying in the hospital, . . . the window was facing the hill. . . . Every day I could hear the staccato shooting of machine guns. . . . I could see a head, or a mother holding a baby, and then after the gunfire they disappeared [down the hill].

Detroiter Molly Chernow, also captured on film by Ms. Rockwell, said her first encounter with Eli in Poland when he led Ms. Chernow's group through Holocaust sites, "was like meeting a rock star because his story really resonated with me and inspired me." When she approached Auschwitz–Birkenau for the first time, Ms. Chernow was in a full-blown panic attack. Eli walked up to her and gently said, "Look at me, I'm not crying. This is a great day, I survived!" As Molly explained, there was something about Eli that was unusual for someone who had been through such horrors: "I would call it his zest for life."

And this optimism and happiness following a childhood characterized by extreme adversity set Eli apart from others. As Eli explained in 2008:

> My wounds have healed but scars remain. I accomplished what I wanted. This year I will turn 82. I'm married happily for 59 years. I have two wonderful children, five grandchildren and one great-grandson; the second is on the way. Three generations born and raised from the ashes of the Holocaust. Today I'm the happiest man in the world. My life is a continuing defeat for Hitler and the Nazis who hoped to destroy the entire Jewish people, but they did not succeed, because 'Am Israel Chai'—the Jewish nation is alive.

Eli was also a visionary. He was certain that he could help change the world by reducing bigotry, genocide, and hate—if only his personal story, and those like his, could become known. That is why, after the initial publication of *A Cup of Honey,* he devoted his life to sharing his story with others and imploring the younger generation to help Eli improve the world. As Eli appealed to Tufts University students in 2010: "This is your responsibility now. Make sure that genocide never happens again. Speak out."

And Eli's life's mission was a success: he did make a difference. He inspired many who read his book and heard him speak to turn their new awareness of the intimate horrors he and so many others suffered during the Holocaust into a calling to prevent it from happening again. After *A Cup of Honey* was published, I received telephone calls, letters, and emails from individuals I did not know who told me how Eli had inspired them to reduce hatred in their communities around the world. Googling Eli's name over the years revealed page after page of commentary from individuals on blogs, news stories, and in other publications from all over the world chronicling the ways in which Eli touched people's lives.

Tour participant Dr. Shari Rogers was so moved by how Eli, despite his losses and hardships, lost neither hope nor his humanity that she founded "Spill the Honey," an organization made up of Jewish American and African American activists who believe that the experiences of both groups are connected and should be used to fight genocide. Stories about Eli's extraordinary impact on those whom he reached can be seen in filmmaker Allyson Rockwell's documentary, aired on Public Television, *Eli's Story: Inspiring Future Generations.*

In 2005 Eli met Miami residents Rossana and Alberto Franco and Mexicans Simon and Michelle Galante in Poland, where he led their March of the Living trip to commemorate the 60th anniversary of the liberation of Auschwitz. They called Eli a "true contemporary hero that touched the deepest membranes of our hearts," and declared that he had changed them forever. "We came back to our homes as different people, our daily life problems put in perspective." Determined to help Eli with the "important task of informing the world of what transpired," the Francos and the Galantes decided that Spanish language speakers should have access to the story, and they spearheaded the Spanish translation and publication of *A Cup of Honey.*

After Eli's story moved them to tears on their first visit to Israel and Yad Vashem in 2009, Boston philanthropists Bill and Joyce Cummings similarly felt their lives had been changed forever, in that they had "gained a new understanding of history and how injustice corrodes the most cherished values of society." The non-Jewish couple first decided to channel their new insights into the development of educational programming to eliminate genocide. They donated one million dollars to Tufts University and founded the interfaith "Cummings/Hillel Program for Holocaust and Genocide Education at Tufts University," which they conceived as a model program in Holocaust and genocide education, and which today supports visits of prominent speakers to the Medford, Massachusetts campus and an annual nonsectarian trip of 20 Tufts students to Rwanda. Later Bill and Joyce Cummings, "seeing the remarkable impact of genocide education on Tufts students," were inspired to expand the program and founded the "Institute for World

Justice," which funds international programs to combat prejudice, hatred, racism, anti-Semitism, homophobia, social inequality, and intolerance.

* * *

BUT HAVE ANY OF THESE EFFORTS HELPED reduce anti-Semitism or helped rid the world of hatred and killing? I think it is fair, during the year of the 70th anniversary of Eli's liberation from Concentration Camp Ebensee and the end of World War II, to ask the question. What would Eli say; how would he answer? Along with his family and many of his close friends, I was heartbroken when Eli died on May 29, 2012, after an illness. So we are not able to ask Eli the question. But I knew Eli well, having spent years with him probing his life experiences as well as his worldview. I think I can propose an educated guess.

There is no doubt that anti-Semitism has not gone away—not just in far off countries, but here in the United States as well. Anti-Semitic incidents so far for the first half of 2015 alone are alarming. The Anti-Defamation League and the Institute for Jewish Policy Research in Britain provide lengthy detailed listings of all known incidents. Just to mention a few: On January 9, two days after the Charlie Hebdo attacks, four Jewish men were killed by a man who stormed a Kosher supermarket in Paris, took shoppers hostage, and held them there, terrified, while he uploaded gruesome video footage of his carnage onto the Internet to incite other attacks in

Paris. In Brasilia, Brasil, on February 4, anti-Semitic posters hung in the city referred to Jews as murderers, thugs and criminals. On February 14, a gunman opened fire at the Great Synagogue in Copenhagen, Denmark, killing Dan Uzan, a Jewish community member who was a volunteer guard at a Bat Mitzvah party and injuring two police officers who prevented the gunman from entering the party.

On March 14, three swastikas were spray painted in a Jewish fraternity house at Vanderbilt University, and on April 25, swastikas, personal slurs, and insulting epithets were spray painted outside a Jewish fraternity house at Stanford University. On March 17, a Jewish man wearing a Star of David necklace was attacked in a St. Polten, Austria, shopping center by a group of men who taunted him with anti-Semitic insults and then attacked him. In Johannesburg, South Africa, on March 21, three Jewish teenagers wearing Kippot, or head coverings, were assaulted at a shopping mall by three men while one of the men shouted: "You f★★★ing Jew and your f★★★ing people are killing our innocent children."

On April 5, at a soccer game in Amsterdam, Holland, soccer fans chanted anti-Semitic slogans such as "My father was in the commandos, my mother was in the SS, together they burned Jews, because Jews burn the best!" On June 24, the monument commemorating the more than 33,000 Jewish victims of the Babi Yar massacre in Kiev, Ukraine was desecrated with spray painted swastikas for the fifth time in about a year.

In France alone, anti-Semitism, having "metastasized via thousands of web sites and social media," has become so rampant that many French Jews are leaving France. In 2014, 50,000 Jews made inquiries to the Jewish Agency for Israel about moving there, according to Marie Brenner's recent *Vanity Fair* article in the August 1915 magazine edition titled "The Troubling Question in the French Jewish Community: Is It Time to Leave?" Efforts to stem the metastasis through Holocaust education are stymied—according to Ms. Brenner, when public schools in France make an attempt to teach about the Holocaust, "Jewish students are insulted, classrooms are vandalized, books are defaced and fights break out . . ."

Chillingly, anti-Semitism and Holocaust denial has become well organized. On April 18, 2015, the *Daily Mail* newspaper in the United Kingdom revealed that a secret meeting and rally, held at London's Grosvenor Hotel, was attended by over 100 neo-Nazis and Holocaust deniers from Europe, the United States, and Canada. The article quoted anti-fascism and anti-racism *Searchlight Magazine's* editor/publisher Gerry Gable warning: "This is the biggest and most significant meeting of Holocaust deniers that Britain has ever seen. It is a very worrying development."

Despite all the efforts at Holocaust education, worldwide Holocaust awareness and acceptance is minimal. In May 2014 the Anti-Defamation League released a global study of attitudes and opinions about Jews in more than 100 countries. The study, conducted by Anzalone Liszt Grove Research, one of the most respected opinion research firms in America, resulted in 53,100 interviews among individuals 18 years and over. The results? Only 54 percent of respondents had heard of the Holocaust, but only 33 percent had heard of it *and* believed it has been accurately described by history. Among those who had heard of the Holocaust, 32 percent believed that it is either a myth or that it has been greatly exaggerated. In the Middle East/North Africa, that figure is 63 percent. Age is an important factor in Holocaust awareness. Only 48 percent of individuals younger than age 35 were aware of the Holocaust, compared to 61 percent of individuals 50 years and older.

There is no doubt that many places in the world in 2015 are very dangerous, anti-Semitism aside, and that hatred, violence and, yes, genocide are all too real and present. Genocide, defined in 1948 by the United Nations Convention on the Prevention and Punishment of the Crime of Genocide (Genocide Convention), means the intentional destruction of a national, ethnical, racial or religious group. Familiar past genocides took place against Armenians (1915-1918) and in Bosnia (1992-95), Cambodia (1975-79), East Timor (1976-2000), Rwanda (1994), Sudan (Darfur) (2003-05) and Ukraine (1932-33). According to *Genocide Watch*, in 2014 eleven countries were in stage nine, the extermination stage, of what it has identified as the ten stages of genocide development. These include South Sudan, Sudan, Syria, Burma/Myanmar, Somalia, Afghanistan, Pakistan, North Korea, Ethiopia, Nigeria and Iraq. *Minority Rights Group International,* in a 2015 release, identified additional peoples under threat of genocide in the Democratic Republic of the Congo, the Central African Republic and Yemen. Victims include ethnic and religious minorities (and, surprisingly, in some case majorities) as well as political opponents.

Even in the face of the continuing presence of vicious anti-Semitism and worldwide genocide, I believe Eli would be proud of his efforts to educate the world about injustice. And, 70 years after his liberation from Ebensee, he would recognize the world as a very different place. As historian Deborah Lipstadt wrote in her op-ed piece in the *New York Times*, on August 20, 2014, differences between then and now are "legion," in that when there is an incident of anti-Semitism today, ". . . officials condemn it. This is light-years away from the 1930s, when governments were not only silent but complicit."

And, contrary to 70 years ago, with the advent of the Internet and social media, even small-scale incidents are recorded and posted for dissemination throughout the world. Perpetrators can now be located and are brought to justice by governments, especially in the West, that strongly condemn and prosecute acts of anti-Semitism. Many governments sponsor education programs to teach the young about anti-Semitism and other forms of bigotry and hatred. Also, as Dr. Lipstadt has pointed out, unlike the 1930s we know how incidents can escalate, and "Jews today are resolute in their determination of: 'Never again.'"

Eli's hard work has also helped in the largely successful worldwide effort to educate the public about genocide. Teaching about mass suffering did not even begin until after the Second World War, or, to be precise, after the Holocaust, because of the world's horror at the attempt by the Nazis to completely destroy European Jewry. After the Holocaust, Universities and private organizations started programs in Holocaust Studies that have morphed into widespread Holocaust education programs that now are also included in primary and secondary school curricula across the United States. As the *International Holocaust Remembrance Alliance* has pointed out, it is only due to the world's investigation of the Holocaust, considered the world's "paradigmatic" genocide, and the dedication of scholars to Holocaust studies and the personal stories of survivors, that the whole field of genocide studies has developed, and numerous past and current atrocities have been identified and continue to be documented.

As the Task Force for International Cooperation on Holocaust Education, Remembrance and Research has suggested, these studies are considered critical to exposing the dangers of abuses of government power; the ramifications of racism, bigotry, and stereotyping; the terrible consequences when modern governments use technology and bureaucracy to implement destructive policies against citizens; and the risk of remaining silent and indifferent in the face of oppression. For these reasons, organizations, educational programs, governments, think-tanks, conferences, and museums worldwide are dedicated to the study and eradication of genocide. And, unlike the 1930s and early 1940s, perpetrators of these atrocities may now be brought to justice, because in 1948 the act of genocide became an international crime under the Genocide Convention.

★ ★ ★

I ALSO AM CERTAIN THAT ELI would not want his death to mean the end of his story and its important message of survival and the resilience of humans in the face of evil. Eli spoke often about his fear that once survivors were no longer available to document their stories personally, the Holocaust deniers would become empowered. Clearly, survivors' messages need a new outlet.

The deputy director of the Auschwitz–Birkenau State Museum, Andrzej Kacorzyk, recognizes this as a "moment of passage;" a "passing of the baton." He noted that at the 60th anniversary of the Camp's liberation a decade ago, 1,500 survivors attended; yet this past January, the 70th anniversary, only 300 attended, and most were in their 90s or over 100 years old. Pawel Sawicki, the museum's chief spokesman, noted that as the baton passes, the museum's displays will change focus. Previously the displays concentrated on "demonstrating the huge scale of the murders at the camps—giant piles of eyeglasses and battered luggage and mountains of human hair." Those displays will remain, but with the survivors largely gone, it is necessary to augment them with individual stories.

And it is through the telling and retelling of individual stories that Holocaust educators can best connect the student to the subject. Lisa Reid, an educator in Great

Britain, explained in *The Guardian*: "Showing my students a photograph of a thousand pairs of shoes is not as powerful as showing my students a single pair. Allowing the students to discover the story behind the shoes makes for a much stronger connection. . . . A family name, a mum and dad, brothers and sisters all tell the story . . . allowing students to empathize with the victims and most importantly, learn from the horrors of the past."

Eli's captivating voice may no longer tell his story, but *A Cup of Honey* can and does. After being out of print for fifteen years, the book is reborn thanks to Kenzi Sugihara and the wonderful team at SelectBooks in New York City. In 2011, Eli wrote in the *Jerusalem Post*:

Sometimes I am asked why it's important to continue all this activity. 'Haven't we done enough?' they ask. But when I meet groups of young people or travel around the world and tell my story, I am confronted both by a willingness and a hunger to listen and learn. . . It is vital to learn about the darkest chapter in human history; a chapter in which our bonds as human beings and our faith in humanity were tested to their limits, and all too frequently did not stand the test. . . . We must ensure that the Holocaust remain in the consciousness of people everywhere, and will never be forgotten.

—SEPTEMBER, 2015
Baltimore, Maryland

PART ONE

Dear and Sweet Childhood

I was born in 1928. My name was Lazer Hershenfis, but my parents called me Lyzerke or Lazorek. Like most other Jewish families in Radom, then a small city in Poland, we were very poor. My parents, my two brothers and my sister shared with me a tiny cocoon-like apartment with only one room. I was the *mezunek,* the youngest child in the family, happy and protected.

Everybody always told me that I was adorable. My left cheek had a permanent red spot on it from all the pinching. I had a round face, a stocky body and black hair. I loved playing soccer or other ball games with my friends, most of whom liked to take me home afterwards to their parents. Adults found me polite and charming. I always addressed them with respect. "Yes, Mrs. Borenstein, we will take care not to use the restaurant window as a soccer goal. You have my word." Most parents thought I was a good influence on their children.

My father, Israel, whom everyone called "Srul," had a small leather business; he cut raw leather and sold it to shoemakers for shoes and boots. My father's "shop" was located in the front section of our tiny apartment, on the first floor of a three-story brown brick building.

A serious, intense man, my father was completely in charge at our house. He looked into your eyes as he spoke to you, and used his hands to help him communicate. He was stubborn and totally honest. He would repeat a message several times to ensure that his listener understood. If someone cheated him in a business deal, he would become red with rage. The only person who could calm him down was my mother.

My mother, Rivka, was beautiful. She had deep-set, big brown eyes that were always smiling. She wore her long black hair in a bun. She was well-known in the community as a healer, and was called upon often when a neighbor was sick with a cold. People in our neighborhood could not afford doctors or medication. When they caught colds or suffered with fever, my mother's old-fashioned remedies were what our neighbors sought.

Once or twice a week, most often in the winter, I would hear a knock at the door and a frantic neighbor would enter our home begging my mother to immediately come to their house to "set *bankies*" on a feverish back. It was always an utter emergency, and it was usually late at night.

"Rivkale, you must come quickly. My poor husband is suffering terribly," a neighbor would plead.

My mother would stop what she was doing and grab the *bankies*. If it were not too late, she would also grab me and sometimes my sister, throw on our warm, woolen, second-hand coats, and rush us through the snow-covered cobblestone streets to the neighbor's house.

Bankies were thick glass cups with a rounded edge. My mother would pour purple spirits in a ceramic bowl and light a candle. She then dipped a cotton-covered stick into the spirits, placed the wet cotton over the candle and quickly swirled the burning cotton stick around inside the *bankies*.

She then would slap the open end of the *bankies*, now filled with moist, hot, medicated air, onto her patient's back, three at a time, aiming directly for the lungs. My mother was an expert at this because she was so fast. Whoosh! Whoosh! Whoosh! In seconds the *bankies* were stuck to the patient's back by suction—up to 18 at one time.

This procedure was believed to provide healing, and in our neighborhood my mother was famous for performing it. She was nicknamed the *bankies shteleren,* or the *bankies* setter.

My mother also was famous as a splinter surgeon. In my city, floors, usually wood, were scrubbed daily with water. We could not afford rugs to cover the rough floors, and in the hot Polish summers, children wore no shoes. We got splinters in our feet. The women scrubbers also got splinters in their fingers. This was terribly painful. I know this, not because I ever scrubbed a floor, but because the women appeared at our door so often seeking my mother's help. Their faces revealed their pain.

My mother had special needles that she kept in a gray ceramic box inside our cupboard. With these needles, she performed "surgery" on our neighbors' feet and hands. Whereas the *bankies* were pulled out most often in the winter, the splinter box was usually opened during the summer, and there were many months when we received patients every day.

Some patients had special motives for seeking my mother's services. One patient, whose name was Rochele, a cook in a local restaurant, was short, fat and not very pretty, but she was in love with my older brother, Mayer. Mayer was handsome, and well known as a good soccer player. He played the goalie on the "Gviasda" team. Mayer, of course, was not at all interested in Rochele. Often, Rochele came to our home at exactly the moment Mayer returned from work.

Mayer first tried to ignore her, but Rochele did not stay away. Next, Mayer tried to make up excuses why he had to leave. Nothing kept Rochele from our house. In fact, she even cooked foods that were Mayer's favorites, such as fried chicken livers and onions, and brought them with her as a way to attract his attention. In desperation, Mayer tried to be rude to her, hoping at least Rochele would stop appearing at our house. This behavior infuriated my mother, who felt sorry for the homely girl.

"Mayer, why do you hurt her so?" my mother asked him.

"She gets on my nerves, Mama," came the answer. The conversation grew into an argument.

"Shame on you!" my mother replied angrily, and Mayer left the house.

The next day, Rochele again appeared at our home. This time, she had invented a novel excuse to be at our home at the very moment my brother returned from work.

"Rivkale, I need your help," Rochele pleaded with my mother. "I think I have a splinter in my finger."

Smiling, my mother said, "A big one or a small one?"

"I don't know," was the answer, "but it hurts."

My brother, who had come inside and begun to eat his lunch at the table, tried hard not to laugh.

My mother took one look at the finger, and realized right away that there was no splinter. With one frustrated glance at Mayer, my mother said: "I see no splinter, but I will clean your finger with spirits."

Mayer, no longer able to control himself, started to laugh and ran out the back door of the house. Humiliated, Rochele's fat face turned red, and she ran sobbing out the front door. That was the last we saw of Rochele as a splinter patient. But from then on, my sister and I wondered about the true motive of any young woman who came to our house for "splinter removal."

 è

My parents, especially my mother, spoiled me. Lunch for my family usually consisted of some kind of meat. In my house, you could not be healthy if you did not eat meat once a day. As a child, I refused to eat any kind of meat, and this was a big problem for my parents. They tried all kinds of techniques to persuade me to eat meat, but the more they tried, the more stubborn I became. This really bothered my mother. She was convinced that I might wither away if I did not eat properly.

One day my mother came up with an idea.

"Lyzerke, I will fry you a cutlet. Will you eat it?"

"It depends," I answered her, skeptically. I knew she was up to something. I was pretty good at predicting when my mother was going to pull a food trick on me. This doesn't mean I was brilliant — she usually tried some sort of trick at every meal. But this one was new. My mother knew I loved fried food. But the question was, what was she going to put inside? Potatoes? I loved potato pancakes.

"What kind of cutlet, Mama?" I asked her, a little worried.

"You will like it, darling," she assured me.

By the time lunch was ready, the whole house smelled like I imagined it must smell in heaven. I couldn't wait to eat. With the first bite I knew I had been tricked, but it didn't matter. The taste of the meat my mother had hidden inside the cutlet was camouflaged, and, if I closed my eyes for a few seconds, and imagined hard enough, it even tasted like a potato pancake.

From then on, my mother made me a special cutlet very often for lunch. Of course, this was no easy task. We had no grinder, and the meat had to be chopped by hand on a wooden board. The chopping alone took plenty of time. She did this chopping and frying in addition to the preparation of the rest of the meal for the family. Only for me was she willing to work so hard.

My mother was loving and kind. When I was two and a half years old, shortly after I was weaned from my mother's breast, our neighbor became ill and could not breast-feed her own baby. Without hesitation my mother volunteered as wet-nurse. And she continued to feed and even care for the baby during the mother's illness, which lasted at least a year. The baby had to be carried around in a brown wool fringed scarf, which my mother attached to her body. My mother had her hands full with her own family, yet she cared for this child as if it were her own.

My father did not spoil me as my mother did — he was usually too busy working or praying. I was careful not to do anything that bothered or upset him. Once when I was nine or 10, my family was visiting relatives who lived near us in Radom. The children played cards all afternoon, while the grown-ups talked and sipped glasses of tea. After we had finished playing cards, I decided I must have them. They were decorated with beautiful, colorful figures. I had never seen cards so lovely. When no one was watching I stuffed the deck into my trouser pocket, and soon afterwards I left with my parents. A little later, the cards fell out of my pocket and my father saw them. He knew everything that was happening in our house.

"Where did you get those cards?" my father said, his voice rising. "Did your cousin Lipa give them to you?" I knew that this was a question designed to provoke me into a lie, and I did not answer him.

"Go back tomorrow and return those cards," my father demanded. "Explain that you took them by mistake and be sure to apologize." I did as I was told, no matter how embarrassed I felt, but I knew that my father would continue to be angry until I demonstrated I had learned a lesson.

My father's shop was separated from our living quarters by a purple flowered curtain that my mother replaced only for the holidays. The holiday curtain was white with a floral and leaf design, and I helped her change it by holding the stool upon which she stood to reach the string that held it to the ceiling.

My whole family lived behind that curtain, in a space that measured only about 90 square feet. We had little furniture. The main piece was a brown-stained cupboard that contained all our clothes, the needle box and the *bankies*. On top of the cupboard rested our small, treasured collection of books. In one corner of the room, two single wooden beds met each other in an "L" shape.

Under the beds were storage areas for potatoes and onions, which my father bought by the sack. I crawled under the bed when my mother needed some potatoes or onions for her cooking. She would say to me, "Lyzerke, I need a few *cartofels* (potatoes)."

My father shared one of the two beds with my brother, Abush, and my mother shared the other with my sister, Chaya. I shared with my oldest brother, Mayer, a small folded cot called a *lezak*, that was stored during the day under my mother's bed in the corner of the room. We slept on canvas-covered mattresses that were filled with straw. After a year, the mattresses would become hard and uncomfortable. My father went to the market to buy new straw and we would refill the canvas bags. It was an irresistible pleasure for me to fall into one of these newly stuffed mattresses. My mother yelled at me, "Stop spoiling the mattress, Lyzerke," while I jumped and jumped.

It was difficult to sleep at night on these beds because they were crowded, even though I was little, and even though I could sink into my own feather-filled pillow and under a thick feather-filled blanket. There was no "bedtime" for me, the youngest one, because in a one-room apartment our bedroom served also as the living room (and the family room, the kitchen, and the closet). If I became tired before the rest of the family, I would fall asleep on my mother's bed. When the family prepared to sleep, my mother would lift me gently into my own bed.

In another corner of the apartment sat a large wooden table on which my sister Chaya and I did our homework and my family ate meals. My mother cooked meals on our wood and coal stove that sat in a third corner of the apartment. When I became old enough, about eight, my mother allowed me to fetch the coal for her from the coal man.

I would take a big basket to the neighborhood *kojlen sklad* or coal yard. My mother had taught me how to distinguish the real coal from black stones that sometimes were hidden in the coal piles that blanketed the yard. I picked up the pieces and put them into the platform scale to be weighed. I placed the coal carefully into the basket so none of it dropped on the ground. The coal was so heavy it took me a long time to reach home, though it was only a few blocks. I had to stop to rest every few minutes, and when I walked with the coal, I had to hold the basket in front of me with both hands. My mother stood outside waiting for me, and when she saw me approaching, she came towards me to take the heavy basket from my hands.

The meals my mother prepared on our stove were a major production, and each day brought an adventure. Every morning, my mother stopped at the Rychul Market, an outdoor market near our house. If I did not have to go to school, I would accompany her. I loved these trips to the market. We would first go to the cheese and butter section. There we would select a heart-shaped white cheese that was wrapped in wet linen. We also would buy some butter that the farmer had wrapped in green leaves. But my favorite was the sour cream. The farmer would pour the thick white sour cream from his heavy, brown pottery jar into my mother's glass jug, which she carried in our straw boat-shaped bag.

We proceeded to the vegetable section, where my mother would pick the ripest red tomatoes, cucumbers, and wonderful green onions. My mother knew I loved to eat the onions with the sour cream. She also selected from the farmer large, fresh, red radishes.

Finally, we approached the bread section, where my eyes would scan the varied selection of breads until they found the fresh raisin bread, which I loved. "Here it is, Mama," I would exclaim to her excitedly. My mouth started to water with anticipation as the baker cut the loaf for us. My mother allowed me to eat a piece of bread right there.

When we arrived home, my mother began to cook. Chaya helped, and I sat watching—I was not allowed to interfere. Meals were not easy to prepare. Everything had to be made by hand. We did not have a refrigerator, so we could not keep leftovers — my mother had to prepare exactly the amount we would eat for each meal.

We had no running water. My father brought buckets of water into the house each day from the neighborhood well located outside in the courtyard. Sometimes I helped pump the water from the well.

On the holidays, my mother prepared our meals in advance and we stored the food in the cool basement of the house. I would walk down the steps with her into a long, dark corridor that led into a large room. My job was to hold a candle to light the dark stairway. We had a storage closet downstairs in which my mother kept a huge wooden bowl. On Sundays, she washed the laundry in that bowl. But on the eve of the holiday, the same bowl was placed upside down on top of our pre-prepared holiday feast to keep out the mice. I placed big rocks on top of the inverted bowl to hold it in place.

I could smell the arrival of the Sabbath in our home. Friday morning, my favorite day, my mother shopped at the Rychul Market. By the time I returned from school, she would be home, baking in our tiny oven two braided *challah* breads. I loved this bread. My mother developed the habit of baking two small *challah* rolls for Chaya and me, which we were permitted to eat even before the Sabbath.

On Fridays, my mother also prepared chicken soup, home-made noodles and gefilte fish for the Friday evening meal, and, in the winter, a special *cholent* to be served for lunch on Saturday. Slow-cooked like a stew, *cholent* consisted of potatoes, beans, meat, and spices. On Friday afternoons, I carried the heavy pot of *cholent* to the neighborhood bakery. All of our neighbors stored their Saturday meal there, because under our religious laws, we were not allowed to cook on the Sabbath.

How could I recognize our pot the next day when I arrived, along with dozens of neighbors, to fetch our meal? I developed a technique to help me find our pot. When my mother handed me the pot on Friday afternoon, the lid would be wrapped in newspaper and tied with string. I drew, with a little paintbrush dipped in black ink, a few designs of the sun surrounded by several letters "H," which was the first initial of our family name, Hershenfis.

On Sabbath morning, after services in the synagogue, I ran as fast as I could to be the first to arrive at the bakery. It was important to arrive as soon as the pots were taken out from the oven so that I could deliver the pot, steaming hot, to my hungry and grateful family.

I can picture, as if it were yesterday, the preparation for the arrival of the Sabbath. An hour or two before, my mother would begin to prepare the hot water for our weekly bath. Each of us had a turn at the basin, placed behind the curtain for privacy. I then dressed, alongside my father, in my Sabbath outfit, which my mother had laid out neatly on the bed. I wore a white starched shirt and grey trousers, and I put on shoes for the occasion.

We could not afford fancy clothes. But my mother boiled our shirts to make them white, and she mended holes expertly, with patches that made the clothes look like new. She used starch for our clothes, and spent precious money at the neighborhood presser to ensure that our Sabbath clothes were crisp and neat.

At sundown, my father, Chaya, and I gathered around the family table where my mother prepared to light the candles. My brothers were usually not yet home from work. I loved watching my mother light the candles. We had beautiful silver candlesticks, a wedding gift to my parents. Just at the moment of sundown, my mother lit the candles. Standing tall and proud above the candlesticks, my mother formed two imaginary circles in the air with her hands, and put her hands to her face. She whispered the Sabbath blessing softly to herself. I stood silently watching my mother in the glow of the candles' light, and felt enormous love and respect for her as she brought into our home the spirit of the Sabbath. When she finished the blessing, her eyes were usually wet. Although I never asked why she cried as she quietly recited the blessing, I believed as a boy, and still believe today, that she cried because she felt she was talking to God.

After the candles were lit, my father and I left for

Friday evening services in Rabbi Usher's *shul*, only a five minute walk from our home. I was proud to accompany my father and felt grown-up to be permitted to carry the family prayer book in my right hand. I held onto my father's hand with my left hand as we walked, along with our neighbors, down the cobblestone street to our *shul*.

When we arrived home from services, the family was waiting. My mother had placed her two beautiful *challah* breads, covered with a hand-embroidered white cloth, on the table, along with a bottle of our homemade wine, the burning candles, and a heavy silver *kiddush* cup. The table was set only for Mayer and Abush, my father and me. There was not enough space in the room to pull the table out from the corner. My mother and sister, when they were not serving the meal, ate a few feet away at the leather shop's worktable, which had been cleaned and covered with a white tablecloth.

At the end of the meal, my family enjoyed singing songs, with my mother leading. My mother sang all the time. She sang while she worked around the house, and as she rocked us when we were little. Her singing influenced us all, especially me. When old enough, I began to sing in the synagogue choir. Eventually, I became one of the soloists. Everyone told me I sang beautifully, and I decided I would become a cantor.

Holidays were exciting. My family began to prepare for the most important holidays months in advance, when my father would bring home a live goose. He put the goose in a closet in the courtyard behind our house. It was my job to help feed the goose every afternoon. My father and I placed his feed into a bottle and took it to the closet. The goose, hearing us approach, would start honking loudly. As my father held the goose, I poured the feed down his throat.

Just before the holiday, my father took the goose to the slaughterhouse. This made me very sad. The goose had become my friend. I knew better than to argue with my father, however, and I buried my sadness deep inside my heart.

The goose provided us with meals for three days. My mother rendered the fat of the goose, and she used the fat for days, preparing wonderful, rich-tasting dishes.

❧

When I turned 10, I was allowed to join a youth movement called B'nai Akiva. The members of the movement were my age and we were the best of friends. We shared many activities together and wore special uniforms when we met on Friday afternoons after school.

B'nai Akiva boys and girls talked all the time about Palestine. We shared a dream that we would all go there one day. We imagined it was a romantic place with sand dunes, palm trees and camels, the land of the Jewish people. We sang Hebrew songs about a place called *Eretz Yisrael,* where all Jews were welcome and belonged.

Here in Radom we had our house and our community, but somehow it did not belong to us. We were different from our neighbors in many ways — in the way we dressed; in our customs and holidays; in the foods we ate and the schools we attended. I played soccer often with Polish boys my age, but these boys reminded us often, especially when they were losing, that we did not belong.

"Jews! Go to Palestine!" they yelled.

My parents wanted, more than anything else, to go to Palestine. They had been nervous about our safety ever since Hitler had begun his campaign to persecute the Jews. Hitler and the reach of his laws were still far away from Poland, but his violently antisemitic propaganda incited our Polish neighbors and increased the danger to us as well.

Also, my parents were religious people. They believed that their lives could achieve spiritual fulfillment only by living in Jerusalem, near where the Holy Temple once stood. Whenever we prayed, we faced east, in the direction of the site of the Holy Temple. We prayed for the reconstruction of the Temple in a Jerusalem where we could live in peace.

Moving to Jerusalem was my parents' lifelong dream and our favorite topic of conversation. We planned to live near the Western Wall, which is the last remnant of the Temple. We wanted to live nearby so that we could walk there to pray. When I was 10, my father arranged for a visa that would allow him to emigrate to Palestine first. He would bring the rest of us a little later. The plan was that he would go to Palestine to "marry" a woman there in a fictional, arranged marriage. It was nearly impossible to obtain a visa to Palestine, and this was the only way it could be done.

In order to execute this plan, my father had to bribe the Polish officials to obtain the necessary documents. My parents sold much of their jewelry and silver to obtain cash for the middlemen. In accordance with the plan, a brother of my mother's who lived in Tel Aviv sent the necessary "request" to initiate the process of arranging a marriage between my father and his new "bride."

We were excited. We prayed to make the dream possible. We would live in Jerusalem. My father would open a leather business. I would learn Hebrew in the morning and play soccer in the sun all afternoon. I would have lots of friends, and we would ride camels in the desert.

When the visa was due to arrive, we anxiously awaited the mailman every day. Finally, we received a message from the British Mandatory Government. But to our great disappointment, the letter contained terrible news.

"Your application for a visa has been denied," the letter said.

My parents were crushed. My mother and Chaya cried for days. My father left the house so no one could see his disappointed face. With that one mail delivery, we lost all hope that we might be able to have a better life. And we had lost our valuables in the process.

I also was upset. I had been bragging for months about leaving for Palestine. My friends were jealous that I would be the first to get there and learn the Hebrew language. I had promised to send them pictures and postcards. I was to have found new friends and a new soccer team, so that when my friends arrived from Poland, they could immediately join my team.

When the visa was denied, I was ashamed. I did not want my friends to know. But they learned the news soon enough from their parents. Everyone in the community knew within hours.

&

I soon forgot my disappointment. I had a friend, Motl, who sang with me in the synagogue choir. One day, when I was visiting Motl to prepare for choir rehearsal, I met Chava, his sister. We quickly knew that we liked each other. We took long walks together, and we discussed plans we might share together in the future.

Chava was exactly my height, and she had black hair that she wore in two thick braids down her back. Her eyes were dark green, and she had beautiful, full, open lips. I liked to watch her lips move as she spoke.

Chava and Motl's father was a locksmith. After Chava and I had known each other for three months, her father gave her a small, metal ring he made in his shop. The ring was not really a girl's ring — it was thick and heavy.

One Saturday afternoon, Chava and I went to the movies together at the Kino Apollo. As we sat in the darkness, I found it hard to concentrate on the movie. I could smell her closeness, and I knew that she was not paying attention either. I reached my left hand over to

Chava and picked up her right hand in mine. It felt soft and her fingers wrapped themselves around mine. As I held her hand, I felt the big ring on her finger.

On the way home, I asked her, "Where did you get the ring, Chava?"

"My father made it," she replied, "but you can see it is too big."

"Let me try it on," I suggested. And she pulled the ring off her finger, immediately slipping it onto mine. It fit perfectly.

"I would like you to have it," Chava said to me, her face turning red. "It will be a token of our friendship."

I was surprised and touched by this gesture, and I looked down at the ring proudly. "Thank you, Chava."

I then reached for her hand, squeezed it, and walked her the rest of the way home.

❧

One day, my friends and I made an amazing discovery that also helped me forget about Palestine. Zalman Borenstein, the father of Leibish, a good friend from B'nai Akiva and my school, owned a restaurant just off the courtyard of my home. It was called "Zalman's Restaurant." This was a very special place, as we soon discovered.

Zalman's Restaurant was a place where mostly Polish people came to eat and to drink vodka or wine. Sometimes this presented problems for the neighborhood because some patrons became drunk and caused trouble.

Often the police were called to settle a brawl. Zalman was a large, tough man who used to beat up and throw out any customer who became violent or refused to pay.

In the back of the restaurant there were two secret rooms. Each had a private dining table and four chairs. A curtained window allowed a small amount of light to enter these tiny dining rooms. We had a feeling that something unusual was happening in these rooms.

One day, as we played in the courtyard, Idale, a friend of mine who was small, quick and an excellent climber, ran to retrieve a soccer ball that had been kicked into the street. After he picked up the ball, he heard loud shouting from one of the two private dining rooms.

Impatient to resume our game, we shouted to Idale, "Come on, hurry up!" But he stood outside the window, motioning for us to shut up and come over quickly.

We couldn't imagine what in the world would be worth seeing at that moment when all we wanted was to continue our soccer game. But we ran over to Idale anyway, guessing there was some drunken brawl going on inside.

"Move aside, let me have a look!" I said to Idale. Through a small opening in the left side of the curtain, I could see a drunken, fat Polish man with his pants hugging his feet. No sooner had I taken a peek, another friend shoved me aside to have a look. We excitedly pushed one another aside in competition to see inside the window.

With the man was a fat woman with long blonde hair and crooked teeth. The woman's face wore many colors. She had bright red lips and cheeks, and her eyelids were caked in blue. She wore a long colorful dress with a low neck and a tight bodice. The Pole and the woman were involved in a loud argument over money.

My friends and I had heard of a kind of woman known in Polish as a *kurva,* or a whore. We were only 10, but we knew that a *kurva* was a businesswoman whose business was sex. We wondered whether we were seeing a *kurva* in action.

After a short time at the window, we ran away laughing, to finish our game. As soon as the game was over, we rushed to find Leibish Borenstein.

I was the first to reach his house, just above the restaurant. I ran up the stairway and rang the bell. Salka, Leibish's sister, opened the door.

"Is Leibish here?" I asked, trying to speak in a low voice so as not to attract the attention of an adult.

"Yes, Lazorek," she answered, giving me a look revealing her suspicion that I and the other boys, whom she could hear laughing at the bottom of the steps, were up to something.

I found red-haired Leibish in the hallway and pushed him into a corner of the room so no one could hear.

"Do you know what we saw through the window of the corner room of the restaurant?" I asked. He did not know. "I do not believe you," he said after I told him. He ran after me down the steps.

We met the rest of the boys outside the restaurant

and they were eager to hear Leibish's reaction to the big story. His reaction was the same. He thought we were up to our usual tricks, and believed not a word we told him.

We decided to stake out the window. It was Sunday, the day off for the Poles, and we were off from school. Our plan was to wait for lunchtime, only half an hour away. We appointed one person as the "inspector" to stand in the dark courtyard passageway and peer inside the window, and two others as guards. One boy would stand outside the gate, and the other at the entrance to the courtyard. The guards were supposed to whistle if anyone came. We let Leibish be the first "inspector."

We took our posts. Those of us without assignments were to wait in the courtyard. We were impatient. After about two minutes, Leibish ran to us laughing so hard that he doubled over. His face was as red as his hair. He could not calm down enough to tell us what he had seen.

So we all ran together to the window to witness the scene of our young lives. A sweaty man with a big mustache sat in one of the chairs. To our amazement, he was wearing no pants, and a blonde woman sat right on top of him in the chair. It looked as if she were riding a horse. At first, we did not know what they were doing in the chair. But after one look at their faces we knew. I now understood why there were unfamiliar girls standing every Sunday at the entrance to Zalman's Restaurant.

We fell to the ground in uncontrollable laughter. Afraid we would give ourselves away if we stayed, we ran, unable to stop the giggles. For Leibish, especially, this was a great discovery. It became our secret. We vowed not to tell anybody. From that day on, we looked forward with excitement to Sundays when, from noon until evening, we took turns "inspecting" the window at Zalman's Restaurant.

ॐ

The routine of our life in Radom was broken each summer, when my parents leased from a Polish farmer a fruit orchard in a village called Rajec Szlachecki, about five miles outside town. We selected our orchard after a springtime orchard-hunt expedition, a walking tour of the countryside. During these spring expeditions, the orchards were in full bloom with fragrant white flowers. My parents could predict, on the basis of the flowering, which orchards would yield a successful harvest.

In the summer, we grew and harvested the apples, pears, plums, and cherries from the orchard and sold them to the dealers at the Rychul Market. This business supplemented my family's small income. It also provided us with a bounty of fruit from which my mother made wine, apple pies and a jam we called *povidla*. Most important to me, it was a big summer adventure.

I traveled with my parents and Chaya to our orchard at the beginning of summer vacation, and we lived in the orchard the whole summer. Our Polish landlord prepared for us a wooden hut with a thatched roof. The first day, my mother would build a stove out of bricks and clay. This stove stood on a wooden stand and contained three burners and even a chimney for the smoke to escape.

I loved the summers in the country. I enjoyed waking up to the smell of the freshly-cut hay and the sound of the farm animals happily preparing for another day in the sun. These sounds were very different from those of the city. In the city, we were accustomed to sounds of the wagon wheels as they negotiated the narrow cobblestone streets. On market day I could also hear the local farmers yelling the virtues of their products.

But in the country it was peaceful and natural. The roosters crowed, predictably, like an alarm clock, when the dawn arrived. They, too, were anxious for the day to begin. Birds whistled beautiful melodies; the staccato sound of the crickets announced the arrival of the sun.

Each morning, when a chicken was ready to lay her fresh brown eggs on my makeshift bed, my mother would capture her under a huge wooden bowl. In a few minutes, my mother removed the bowl, and like a miracle, an egg appeared almost out of nowhere.

I liked to spend time during the days helping the Polish farmer with his work in the fields and with the animals. I held the reins as the horse pulled the metal plow. When I wasn't helping around the farm, I played games with my sister, Chaya, to pass the time until the harvest.

Chaya was a frail girl with brown eyes and long, light brown hair that she wore in braids. She was four years older than I. Her pale face was sprinkled with lots of freckles. She was quiet and good-natured and shared with me anything that was hers.

Chaya and I had a lot in common, even though we had separate friends. We did not attend the same school, but found time to play together when we were in the city. Chaya was proud of me and loved to show me off to her girlfriends.

"This is my lovable little brother!" she would say to them, smiling and pulling me close to her. This would embarrass me a little, and I would try to turn my face away from her so she and her friends could not see me turn red.

But I loved being alone with her. In the country, after we had finished our chores around our hut, we had time to play games or just talk. Our favorite game was called *strulkies*, which we played with five smooth stones found hiding among the rough ones alongside the river bank. It took us time to search for stones of the right shape and size. A perfect one was as rare as a jewel.

The object was to throw the stones together in the air and catch them with the back of the same hand. If you dropped any, you had to pick them up with the same hand that was holding the caught stones. This became very complicated at times and I loved the challenge.

We needed a smooth surface to play, so we took a board, placed it in the middle of a deserted field, and sat on top of it. We sat there for hours playing. My sister usually won — she was an expert at this game, and had larger hands, which gave her an advantage. She was so good that it bored her sometimes to play with me, clearly an inferior player. But I begged her to continue, and she always did.

At suppertime, we packed up and ran home from the fields.

"Don't you think Mama is looking for us?" I would say.

"She knows where we are, Lyzerke. But if you are hungry, let's go to eat," she would reply. Chaya knew how I loved the meals of fresh bread, cheese, and butter or onions, radishes, and sour cream that our mother prepared for us in the country.

Another favorite activity was making paper boats. Using a technique Chaya had learned in school, we folded old Polish newspapers into boats of all different sizes. We took our boats down to the nearby stream and raced them along the current. Sometimes the rocks in the stream capsized a boat. I would get so angry I would pound my fists onto the sides of my legs. If we were lucky, to our delight, our boats would sail away with the stream until we could no longer even see them.

We played "catch" with a homemade ball. We made this ball out of old socks that we filled with sawdust and tied with strings.

We loved picking wild blueberries from the forest near our orchards. After a frequent Polish summer rain, huge white and brown wild mushrooms also grew. It was fun to find these mushrooms, and we competed to find the biggest ones. One time we brought mushrooms home and my mother got very upset.

"Throw them away right now, they may be poisonous, and don't you ever take them from the forest again," she shouted. "Go wash your hands, quickly!"

Of course, this scared us and we went immediately to scrub our hands.

The next time it rained I became curious.

"Chaya, let's try to find some mushrooms," I suggested to my sister.

"Are you crazy, Lyzerke? Remember Mama said they are poisonous!" I realized that Chaya was probably right, and we never again picked mushrooms in the country.

Sometimes, we played with the children of our Polish landlord. We played hide and seek in the barn, behind bales of sweet-smelling hay. We played jump rope, singing Polish songs that established a rhythm for the rope. On hot days we went to the river to bathe. The Polish children became our good friends, and sometimes ate meals with us outside our hut.

When harvest time arrived at the end of summer, my brothers and their friends came to the country to help us pick the fruits. They arrived after work in the afternoon, and we picked until dark. They stayed with us at night to guard the orchards from thieves. The fruits we picked were placed carefully into huge straw baskets, and by the next morning, were already on their way to the market.

٭

The summer of 1938 was our last summer in the orchard. The atmosphere in and near Radom was becoming tense. We had leased the orchard as usual, and by late August, we had completed most of the harvest. My mother returned to the city with my sister, leaving my father and me alone to complete the last of the summer's work.

Just before dawn one morning, I awoke to the sound of loud noises just outside our hut. Suddenly, two drunken Poles rushed inside, grabbed my father from his bed next to mine and dragged him outside of the hut while beating him with their fists.

"Bloody Jew," they yelled at my father. "Go to Palestine!"

Frightened and stunned, I jumped out of bed and ran outside to help my father. I began to yell and cry. My father tried to push the men away, but they were huge and vicious; it was impossible to defend himself against their blows. I screamed for help. I saw a wooden board covering our water bucket, and without thinking, I grabbed the board and tried to hit the men who were beating my father. One of them lifted me up with one hand as ·if I were a chicken and threw me in the air. I landed two yards away. The men continued hitting my father until he fell to the ground, bleeding and beaten. Then they ran away.

I found a cloth, dipped it in our water bucket, and gave it to my father to apply to his wounded face. My father was terribly upset and ashamed. He would not look me in the eye and he did not speak to me. We completed

the harvest the following day and never returned to that
place.

ॐ

By the summer of 1939, our lives had changed
dramatically. Rumors were that war was about to begin.
We sensed that bad times were on the way. People
stored food if they could afford to buy it. Prices had
risen for basic staples, such as oil, sugar, flour and jam,
and lines formed for these things in stores. We could not
afford much, especially since we no longer had any
income from the orchard, but my mother did manage to
find some flour and a little sugar for us.

My brothers were employed as tailors for a Jewish
company in Radom. My sister was preparing to return to
work as a day-care provider at a Jewish kindergarten for
girls. I was bored with spending the entire summer in the
city and eager for summer to end and school to begin.

I was to enter the sixth grade at the Piasky Public
School, a local school for Jewish children where classes were
taught by both Jewish and Polish teachers. We learned
secular subjects such as math and geography as well as
religion.

I had enjoyed in particular my Bible class,
especially the story of the Book of Genesis. I was the
school's geography expert, well known among my class-
mates for drawing maps of Africa. I was able to identify
with a different color each country on that continent. I

knew by heart most of the names of the mountains, valleys, and rivers in Africa. My teacher was impressed with my work, and she taped one of my maps on the blackboard as an example for the class.

Several weeks before the beginning of the school year, my mother came to me with terrible news.

"Lyzerke, I am afraid that your school will not open anytime soon."

She explained that all Polish schools were to be closed so that the teachers could report for mobilization in the army. Seeing my shocked and disappointed face, she added, "But with God's will, the problems will be over soon and your school will reopen for you to continue your studies."

Though my mother tried to comfort me and Chaya, who now had no job, I was worried. I had heard terrible stories about the Germans and about the way they were treating the Jewish people in Germany. I heard these stories from German Jewish children who had succeeded in escaping to Poland. These children told us that the Germans had burned their synagogues and their parents' shops. Some Jews, including some of their parents, had disappeared suddenly without a trace.

I did not want to believe these stories, yet I felt frightened. How could a government burn buildings belonging to its own people? Why would anyone burn a synagogue, a house of God? Wars were fought against other governments. Who was there to protect the people against terrible things if not their government? Could our government here in Poland do these things to us? Who would protect my synagogue? My house? My family?

In early August a notice appeared on public bulletin boards throughout Radom and in the newspapers. Volunteers were needed to dig trenches and shelters to protect us against German air attacks. Men were being recruited for service in the Polish Army. I was nervous that my older brother, Mayer, would be called and that I would not see him for a long time. Then, events began to happen so quickly that I ran out of time to be afraid.

PART TWO

Childhood, Very Sad, Dark, and Bitter

September 1, 1939, a Friday, I heard the first siren. My entire family was at home and we ran together with some neighbors to our shelter, located in the basement of our house. I wanted more than anything to go with my friends outside to see the planes flying overhead, but our mothers held us back. As soon as the sirens ended, I took off with some of my friends in search of excitement.

We went to the Apollo movie house, where a lone Polish soldier, positioned on the roof, had been trying to shoot back at the German planes with a machine gun. Trucks and grim-faced soldiers were moving out from the Polish Army's 72nd Regiment Armory, inching slowly toward the main road.

That evening, my mother lit the Sabbath candles as usual and we ate dinner. But our mood was sad. We did not sing our traditional songs that night. As soon as dinner was over, my brothers rushed out to catch the radio news bulletin at our neighbor's house.

The news was alarming. The Germans had indeed

penetrated into Poland and civilians had begun to flee eastward to the Russian border. I did not know it, but my brothers had already planned their escape to the East. A few days later they disappeared, without even saying goodbye to me.

One week later, Friday, September 8, 1939, the Germans entered Radom. I heard a sudden loud buzzing sound and ran outside and down the street. I saw an extraordinary sight. Strange soldiers wearing green helmets and goggles, with submachine guns or rifles strapped across their chests, were entering my city on huge green motorcycles with sidecars.

These soldiers made a real commotion as they traveled along our formerly peaceful cobblestone streets. They were followed by open trucks containing even more soldiers and then — tanks! I could not believe my eyes. As the German soldiers conquered our city, they showed they hated the Jewish children. All the children waved to them as they drove past. But the sight of the strangely dressed Jewish children invited screams and snarls.

This Friday was different from any other Friday I ever knew. My parents locked our door early in the day. At night, we ate a quick dinner in silence. My mother somehow had baked the *challah* but had not prepared the usual festive meal. The air was heavy and I could feel enormous tension, fear, and dread. I wanted badly to understand what was happening, but I was afraid to ask questions and my parents did not volunteer any answers. We went to sleep without pulling out the folded bed. With my brothers gone, my father and I shared one of the wooden beds.

The next morning, instead of going to the synagogue with my father, I went with a few friends to Rynek Square, in which the City Hall was located. Most of the shops around the square were closed. The usual crowd of people that milled about in the square was absent.

Then I saw it. High above the magistrate's building, hanging from a large flagpole, flew a giant red Nazi flag with a black swastika in the center. I had never seen this symbol before, outside of photographs, and I did not completely understand its significance. But the black swastika looked mean and threatening.

A few days later, the German SS — the Gestapo — entered my city. In the morning, my friend Leibish Borenstein and I walked to the main shopping area in Radom, at Zeromskiego Street. Before we reached the shops, our eyes fixed upon a group of sharp-looking officers stepping out of a shiny black convertible and entering a shop. These men wore crisp black uniforms, red armbands with black swastikas, beautiful tall black boots and hats decorated with a skull and crossbones. A skull and crossbones! These men couldn't be pirates — they didn't have pirate clothes on, and there was no place in Radom to anchor a pirate ship! These men were German SS officers! We stared at the car for a long time — fascinated because it was beautiful, clean, and modern.

During the first few months of the occupation, the Germans issued many decrees. Printed in two languages, German and Polish, the decrees were posted on the city bulletin boards. They were signed by the SS Governor of the Radom District. All Jewish schools were forbidden. All Jews over age 10 were forced to wear a white armband with a blue Star of David insignia. Jews were prohibited from entering the main streets and squares in the city during certain hours. Jews were forced to remove their hats whenever a German soldier passed them in the street. Jews could no longer enter theaters or cinemas.

These restrictions had an immediate impact. I lost all hope that my school might reopen. I needed to find something to do to pass the time. Before the war, I had enjoyed going with my friends, Leibish or Zelig, to Kino Apollo. We loved American western films. Our favorite cowboy heroes were Tom Mix and Ken Maynard.

It cost 25 groshy to enter the movies. My parents could not afford to let me go, but my brother, Abush, would always give me some change so that I could accompany my friends. Sometimes Abush even took me himself to the movie house. Now that I was forbidden to enter the Apollo, it upset me.

The armband was another problem, not because I felt ashamed to wear it, but rather because it identified me as a target for the Polish boys. I worried constantly about being attacked. My Polish neighbors were encouraged by the Germans to pick fights with us. Before the war, these Polish boys had been our playmates on the soccer field and on the playgrounds. We felt hurt and sad that our former friends would so quickly and eagerly become our persecutors.

The High Holidays of 1939 came shortly after the German occupation, but we had little to celebrate. Many Jewish people had been forced out of their jobs. My father was self-employed but he had few customers, as most Jews could not afford new shoes. My brothers were gone. We had little income, and found it hard to afford food.

The Germans issued a decree that we would not be allowed to attend religious services in our synagogues. This was too much for my father. On Yom Kippur, he decided to defy the German decree by organizing religious services in a nearby school. The plan was simple. He and his friends would worship as usual. We children would serve as "guards," and in the event Germans should approach, we were to warn our fathers so they could escape.

But the plan did not work. Aided by Polish informers, the SS targeted these small gatherings of worshippers. I was standing guard on Vitolda Street Number 3, outside Rabbi Usher's school, where my father was praying with about 20 other men. My friend Idale and I stood near the wooden fence next to the school.

All of a sudden, two German trucks appeared out of nowhere, one empty except for the driver, and the other full of SS soldiers. We rushed into the school to warn our fathers, but were too late. Before the wheels of the trucks came to a complete stop, the SS men jumped down to the ground and ran into the school, their rifles held menacingly in front of them.

"*Alle Juden Raus!*" they yelled. "All Jews outside!"

"*Schnell, Schnell!*" they screamed. "Quickly, Quickly!"

Idale and I stood there trembling as the SS men, using their rifle butts and their booted feet, pushed and kicked our fathers and the other men outside the school, onto the street and into the open trucks. The soldiers ignored Idale and me and we ran outside after our fathers. We saw an awful sight. In the street stood our Polish neighbors and former friends laughing at the awful sight of our humiliated fathers being taken away.

The trucks slowly moved down the cobblestones towards Zeromskiego Street. Idale and I, tears streaming down our faces, ran after them. We hoped to find out where our fathers were being taken, but we could not run fast enough.

Horrified, we ran home to our mothers, who, along with the whole neighborhood, had already heard of the raid. With the other wives, my mother stood trembling in the street all afternoon waiting anxiously for any information about the men.

I also waited outside for my father to return. I was scared that he might be hurt, or even killed. I felt guilty for not having served as a better "guard." I hurt for my dear mother, whom I loved so much. I wanted badly to be able to erase her worry and fear for her husband.

My eyes were glued to the streets. At last, I saw my father walking with some other men up Vitolda Street. He looked beaten, with bruises all over his face and hands. He was black, as though from coal dust, and he walked strangely. I soon discovered why.

The men had been taken to a German army base to unload coal from wagons. They were forced to work there all afternoon on Yom Kippur, the holiest day of the Jewish year. The Germans forbade breaks of any kind as they forced the men to unload coal.

My father needed to use the toilet and requested permission. There were, however, no toilets in the area. An SS guard showed my father where he could relieve himself on the ground, and, after my father finished, the SS man forced him to sit down in his excrement.

My father, a proud and honorable man, was humiliated. When he arrived home that evening, covered with the excrement, he avoided us and would not look into our eyes. Even after my mother helped him clean himself and his clothes, my father was unable to eat the dinner my sister served him. The four of us sat silently, fearing what was going to happen to us.

❧

We worried about my brothers. Where were they? Had they reached safety, or had they been caught? Since they had left, we had heard nothing. Winter was approaching, and some of the young Jewish men who had escaped with my brothers began to return to Radom. They told us that others were trying to get home. Many feared the cold Eastern winters more they did than the Germans.

The Germans began to ration our food and coal. In short supply even before the rationing, now the Jews were receiving even less of both. My sister Chaya and I had the important job of standing in the line at the bakery to buy our family's meager portion of bread. We huddled together in this line for hours each day in the freezing cold. As I stood in line, I remembered when my mother and I would buy our bread from the farmer who sold it with a smile. Then, we did not wait in line, we could buy as much as we wanted, and the bread was fresh.

Now, it was hard to progress to the front of the line because the Polish customers pushed us and the other Jews to the end. We worried that we would not make it to the counter before the bakery was emptied. Then our family would have no food.

One day, after we managed to purchase our bread ration, I went to Rychul Square, where I had a view of Kozienicka Street. This was the route of the men who were returning from the East. I hoped in my heart that my brothers would appear.

It happened. I saw two familiar figures walking down the street. I wanted to bolt back to my mother to report the wonderful news, but I stopped to make sure that it was really Abush and Mayer. Once certain, I ran as fast as I could, tears streaming down my face, crying, "Mama, Abush and Mayer have returned!"

With my mother behind, I ran back to the square to greet my brothers, glancing back at my breathless mother to make sure she was following me. I reached my brothers first and jumped on top of them, crying and laughing at the same time.

Mayer and Abush were freezing. Their clothes were wet, their noses and cheeks were red and their toes blue. As soon as we reached home, my mother gave them glasses of hot tea to drink and warm clothes to put on. When they had warmed up a little, they began to tell us their story. They had tried to cross into Russia but Russian soldiers had caught and arrested them.

Fearful that they would be sent to Siberia along with many others, my brothers looked for an opportunity to escape from the Russians. They were lucky, because they were among the few who managed to escape. But the experience did not deter them from trying again. For several weeks, my brothers hid in the forest, waiting for an opportunity to cross the Russian border. But it never became any easier to cross, and, frustrated with the increasing cold and lack of food or any way of making money, they decided to return home.

The Germans were arresting those returning from the East on the pretext that they were spies. We had to hide my brothers, not only from the Germans, but also from the Poles, who were informing on those who had returned. But we had no choice except to add them to the list of Radom Jews. This list was compiled by the *Judenrat*, or the Jewish Council, an organization set up to implement German orders concerning the day-to-day aspects of our lives. It was necessary to declare my brothers' presence because we desperately needed additional food rations.

The small amount of food my parents, Chaya, and I were rationed did not satisfy even the four of us, and we needed more now that Mayer and Abush were back home.

Conditions were becoming worse. The winter of 1939–1940 was particularly cold, and we did not always have coal. We substituted wood for coal, collecting it in the streets, the gardens, and from the garbage. Desperate, we collected and burned dried leaves that we sometimes found when the snow melted.

One cold winter day, I was outside with my friend, Sheikeh, trying to find some dried leaves to burn in our stove. Snow lay thickly on the ground, making it almost impossible to find anything dry. I momentarily forgot my near-impossible task and decided to have a little fun.

I turned my back to Sheikeh and began to roll snow into a big, hard snowball. Sheikeh saw me and started to form his own snowball. After a few seconds, Sheikeh saw that my snowball was bigger than his, so he ran over to me and kicked my snowball. Laughing, Sheikeh darted away. I was fast, and took off after him down Vitolda Street. I caught him, and, angry that he had ruined my snowball, started to beat him up. Sheikeh began to cry.

At that moment, a tall young German SS man ran over to us. The German wore a long black coat and a black leather belt that held a pistol in a holster. I saw him approaching, and panicked. I released Sheikeh, and the two of us started to run as fast as we could in opposite directions.

"HALT! HALT! HALT!" the German shouted at me as I ran off. I ignored him and kept running. After a second I realized that the German was running after me. I heard his heavy footsteps, but they seemed to be getting farther away. Was I outrunning him?

Suddenly I heard a loud gunshot. A gunshot? At me? On Vitolda Street? I could not believe my ears. The Poles in the street were also surprised and stopped to find out what all the commotion was. Realizing that the first pistol shot was directed at the clouds but that the second might kill me, some Polish bystanders motioned for me to stop. And I did.

Scared to death, I stood there trembling. The German had a furious look on his face. He walked slowly up to me and grabbed me by the back of the coat. A crowd of Poles started to form around us.

"This Jew beat up a Polish boy. I saw it," the German said to the crowd in German. The people began to discuss among themselves how I could have done such a thing.

One of the Polish men turned to me and said in Polish, "Why did you beat up the Polish boy?"

Realizing that there had been a mistake, I started to cry. I said to the Polish man, "The boy was my friend, Sheikeh. He is a Jew. I was beating him because he ruined my snowball."

The Polish man translated what I said to the German, and the German threw me to the ground and started to walk away. The Poles went back to their activities.

I realized that the danger was over but I could not rise. I lay there on the ground for many minutes, shaking and crying. When I finally got up the inside of my pants was wet.

Shaken and embarrassed, I ran home with my face hidden under my coat. For many days, I was afraid to walk outside.

I hated having to walk in the street instead of on the sidewalk. Everyone else could walk on the sidewalk, and I felt humiliated, singled-out, and self-conscious. Yet it was boring inside. We were forbidden to possess a radio precisely at a time when we longed for news, music, and culture. I felt isolated. I began to fear that the Germans would take over the world.

That winter of 1940 we became hungrier and hungrier. Our food rations were totally inadequate. We ate the same thing every day — potato soup, which my mother would serve as our main meal at noon. Sometimes, she added a little flour to this soup to make it more filling. We were rationed a single slice of bread for breakfast and another for dinner. On the bread, we would spread a little of the jam that my mother had prepared years ago from the bounty of our former harvest.

Weeks passed before we could afford to buy a few grams of meat or chicken. Occasionally we were able to find an egg, which my mother would scramble and then give to Chaya and me to share. Often, my mother would force my sister and me to share her portion of bread. My mother insisted she was not hungry. I did not believe her, but I knew better than to argue.

It became apparent that those of us who could work must find a job, because we desperately needed to supplement our food rations. A black market for food was available to those who had the money. It was not easy to secure a job. For the Jews, jobs in Radom were extraordinarily scarce.

Nevertheless, Mayer and Abush finally managed to find work as tailors in a Jewish-run factory making clothes for the Germans. Their meager earnings, combined with my father's business income, enabled us to purchase a small amount of additional bread and potatoes or a little fat or flour.

There was no work, however, for Chaya or me because we were too young. We came up with an idea that would keep us busy and could provide the family with additional income. The Germans had closed the Radom tobacco factory, and cigarettes had become scarce and expensive. Some boys I knew had learned a method of making handmade cigarettes and the Germans or the Poles would buy them for a few groshy or marks.

I decided that this would become my business, too, and Chaya could help. Abush bought fresh, yellow tobacco leaves from local farmers or at the market. Chaya and I dried the leaves on the stove and cut them into thin strips. We crushed the strips and inserted the crushed tobacco into thin cigarette paper. Abush had bought us a special instrument we could use to pack the tobacco tightly in the paper.

Chaya packed the cigarettes into small boxes for

me to peddle on the street. I stood in the public squares during the hours that Jews were permitted there, and held the box of cigarettes in front of me.

"*Papierosi! Papierosi!*" I yelled out: "Five for 50 groshy!"

I had plenty of customers. The German soldiers especially liked my product. They gave me marks instead of groshy, which I could change at the bank. After a day of business, I usually sold all my cigarettes. Proud, and eager to show Chaya and Mama the money I had earned, I ran home. My mother took some of the money to buy food, coal, or wood. The rest we invested back into the business, and Chaya and I worked on making the next day's supply. Once a week, as a special treat, Chaya and I took a few groshy to buy an ice cream or some candy from Polish shops in the square.

But as winter dragged on, our business began to yield less of a profit. It was cold and wet outside, and I became frustrated waiting for customers who did not appear. My sister and I reluctantly put away the cigarette equipment and again found ourselves with nothing to do.

That winter, my brother's friend Srulik offered me a job in his hat-making factory. Srulik was a well-known hatmaker in town, and he had received many requests from the German civilians living in Radom to manu-facture warm winter hats.

I happily became an assistant to this hatmaker. I worked every day from seven o'clock in the morning until five in the afternoon. It was not monotonous because our hats were custom-made, and each was designed and made differently. For my work, Srulik paid me a few zloty every week. My mother was happy to receive this additional income because it helped to buy food or to keep the house warm.

In about February, 1940, my father's business, which did not attract Polish or German customers, began to fail. He decided it was time for him to find work elsewhere. A neighbor who worked in a shoemaking factory called Pulka offered my father a job as a leathercutter. The income was far less than my father was accustomed to, but at least he was working.

For about a year following that February, those of us who had jobs went straight to work every morning and returned in the evening directly to our homes. We did not walk the streets in the evenings or go out during the weekends for fear of being rounded up by the Germans to shovel snow or to perform other random jobs. On the weekends, I played soccer with my friends in our courtyard if the weather was nice. If it was raining or snowing, my friends and I played cards or dominoes inside our homes. But except for my mother and sister, who shopped for food or supplies during the day, we did not go anywhere in Radom.

❧

In March, 1941, we learned that the Germans were planning to establish a Jewish ghetto in Radom. It became apparent, to our horror, that we had to leave our home. Our home consisted of only one room, but it was safe and warm. I had known no other: from the time I was born, we had lived there. In that one room we slept together, ate together, sang songs together, shared happiness together and suffered together. That room bound us. I knew somehow, when we were forced to leave it, that we would never return as a family.

The Germans gave us one month to find an apartment in the ghetto. Our ghetto was located in a crowded and poor slum neighborhood called Valova. The Poles who lived there were ordered to leave to make way for the Jews. Many Jewish families attempted to trade their homes with Poles from Valova.

In April, my father made arrangements with a Polish family to trade our home on Vitolda Street for theirs. The new home was very different from the one we were leaving. It was a wooden, dilapidated, one-story building located at 26 Shvarlikovska Street. The street was narrow and paved with cobblestones.

We waited until the last possible hour before moving. My father hired a "v" shaped horse-drawn wagon to transfer our belongings. My mother and Chaya packed up everything, including the beds, linens, table, cupboard, pots and pans, and all our clothes. My father and brothers loaded the wagon with our heavier things and I helped carry out the lighter items. Until the final moment, my mother kept busy wrapping our most meaningful possessions carefully in towels and paper and placing them into straw baskets. One by one, she packed our Sabbath candlesticks, her *bankies* and needle box and our *kiddush* cup. I could see her fighting back her tears. She did not want Chaya or me to see her anguish.

When we finished packing, we walked one last time through the apartment. The light blue walls appeared stark and brooding. Our black stove, which we called the *piecyk,* looked lonely. I imagined that the *piecyk,* sitting all by itself in the corner of the room, would feel sad that my mother would not be there any longer to prepare, with its cooperation, our family's favorite things.

My mother could no longer hold back her emotions and broke down, crying and sobbing. I was surprised and afraid by her outburst because my mother was usually so optimistic — she was the one who saw the bright side of terrible events. I tried to calm her.

"Mother, don't cry, we will come back," I said.

But she was inconsolable and my own feelings became too powerful. I turned around in tears and ran out of the room for the last time.

When we arrived at our new place, we discovered, to our dismay, that we had to share the tiny apartment with another displaced Jewish family, the Finkelshteins. The Finkelshteins had paid money to the same Polish family who had supposedly "traded" their apartment for ours. Now there were two families, strangers, who had no choice but to live in the same cramped one-room apartment in the ghetto.

Adjustment to ghetto life was not easy. It was a

strange place where I knew no one. My usual hangouts were off-limits. I could not leave the ghetto to visit them. I completely lost contact with every one of my good friends. Chava and her brother, Motl, went to a smaller ghetto in Radom called Glinice, a place inaccessible to us. I did not have a chance, in the confusion of the last days, to say good-bye. Leibish and Idale also disappeared, probably to another part of my ghetto. Pinchas Mandlebaum disappeared from Radom with his parents. Sheikeh and I lost all contact.

My family suffered badly in the first months of the ghetto. Except for my father, who continued to work for Pulka, none of us was able to find regular work. We had almost no income. We could not afford to buy more than a half loaf of black, dry, tasteless bread each day. My father divided the bread carefully so that each would receive an equal share. We ate this bread at noon, along with a watery soup my mother made from a few half-rotten potatoes and onions. This was our only meal. I felt hungry all the time, but I never complained because I knew that it made everyone else in the family suffer to know that I was hungry.

Jewish organizations were set up in the ghetto to provide a daily supply of food to the poor. My parents were too proud to allow us to receive charitable food supplies. As the days turned to weeks and then months, my mother sold her wedding ring, earrings, necklaces and any other personal jewelry she still had — most of which she had received from her own mother — to scrape up a few zloty to buy additional food. When we had sold everything of any value, we could no longer afford even to buy the black bread.

I was so hungry that I was in no mood to meet new friends or even to play *strulkies* with Chaya. I became depressed, but I forced myself to figure out a way to find any kind of work. Like other young boys, I began to wander through the streets during the day searching for odd jobs. Like others, I looked terrible. I had lost weight, my cheeks were sunken, and my eyes were surrounded by black rings.

Occasionally, I found work. A dentist who was a family friend, Dr. Birenbaum, hired me to clean his chimney. He paid me a few groshy and he gave me some coal to take home to my mother. I worked from time to time for the Germans, who took some ghetto workers every day for work in German installations nearby. They paid us very little, but we were fed a small meal. This helped me, but it was hard to find jobs like these because everyone wanted them.

Our housemates, the Finkelshteins, had an income because Moishele, the father, was employed in the *Judenrat*. They were disturbed by our suffering, and offered every day to loan us money to buy food. My mother, too proud at first to borrow any money, eventually accepted the offer. She promised that, with God's help, we would pay them back.

Conditions were the same for most ghetto residents. Food was in extremely short supply. Everyone searched for some way to obtain it. Ragged-looking, dirty children stood on street corners begging for a piece of bread. Luckier children earned money to buy food by working 12-hour shifts at hard labor.

Many people fainted or starved to death right in the streets of the ghetto. I saw bodies lying in the streets. After a while, I got used to it, and would step over or around a body as if it were a normal thing to do. The horse-drawn black wagon that carried out the dead for burial became a regular sight.

Overcrowded living conditions and improper diet caused typhus and dysentery to spread. Medical supplies were unavailable and people did not recover easily from these diseases.

One day my father became sick with dysentery. He collapsed onto the wooden bed in our apartment suffering from stomach cramps, vomiting, and diarrhea. He could not get out of bed, and had to relieve his diarrhea into buckets that my mother kept by his bed. For four or five days, my father suffered with a terribly high fever.

My mother was convinced that we were going to lose him and prayed all day for a miracle to occur. She did not want my father to be taken to the hospital, no matter how sick he was, because conditions in the hospital were no better than those at home and, in many ways, worse.

On the sixth day, a miracle did occur. My father began to improve, and, within a few days, he got up out of bed. This improved our morale considerably. We believed that we had passed the worst of times and that things could only improve.

We were wrong. Conditions in the ghetto continued to deteriorate. The SS began to raid homes regularly, day and night, in search of particular individuals, usually men, whom they wanted. Often the SS even seized individuals who were not on their list of "wanted men." We knew that victims of these raids either were shot on the spot or were arrested and taken to the Gestapo cellars. We heard that the victims were tortured, and then sent away to concentration camps with names that were strange to me: "Auschwitz" and "Majdanek." We heard that those who were sent away to these places never returned.

I cannot put out of my mind one aspect of these roundups. When the Gestapo came in search of a victim, they were accompanied by a member of the Jewish ghetto police. This special group was set up by the Germans to "maintain order" in the ghetto. Policemen were promised that their families would be "protected" in return for their service as "police." But in reality, these "policemen" acted as agents for the Gestapo, and sometimes carried out beatings and rounded up individuals for deportation or murder by the Germans. I wondered how these "policemen" could collaborate with the Germans against their own friends and relatives.

I feared that my brothers would appear on the list of wanted men. I could not sleep at night, worried that the SS would take them away. One night, just before bedtime, we heard loud shouting outside and then heavy footsteps. Terrified, I started to shake. It was the Gestapo, and they were soon inside our home searching for certain men.

Mayer and Abush were not the target of the search that day. Nevertheless, terrified also, my brothers dove underneath the beds and remained there until the SS had left.

Things seemed to improve a little after that search. My brothers were able to find work as tailors in a workshop set up to provide clothing for German civilians who had settled in Radom. Workshops in the ghetto provided a meager salary in return for skilled work. Workers were required to labor hard — 12 hours a day, seven days a week. As difficult as the working conditions were in the factories, those who managed to become employed were considered lucky. The income, no matter how small, helped provide desperately-needed food.

More important, skilled workers were protected from the deportations that were beginning to take place regularly. These deportations were to be avoided at any cost. We were not sure where deported people were being taken, but rumors spread that they were going to work camps, and that they did not return from these places.

My mother and sister could not find work because they were unskilled. They would sit at home all day, worried about being discovered and taken away. Our housemate, Esther Finkelshtein, a pretty girl with brown eyes and black hair, about 18 years old, found a job in a German army clothing supply base. The German *Wehrmacht* had confiscated the former Radom tobacco factory on the outskirts of the city, and had turned it into the *Armee Fürsorge Lager* or AFL. Esther reported to us that the working conditions at the base were not too harsh, and that the German army provided a big lunch to the workers.

Just before Christmas, 1941, Esther arrived home and told my mother that the clothing department of the AFL needed some young workers over the age of 15. Would she agree to allow me to apply? My mother would let me apply for the job, but there was a problem. I was only 13.

When I heard about this job opening, I was determined to figure out a way to get it. And Esther was determined to help me. Esther knew some Polish workers from the AFL with connections in the Radom Municipal Records Office. Through these connections, Esther arranged for my birth date to change in the birth records book. From then on I became two years older. The German who was in charge of the clothing storage warehouse at the base, a red-faced, heavy sergeant who was called "Czervony" or "Red," did not question the fake date of birth on my job application. He was fond of Esther because she was charming and attractive and an efficient worker. Her recommending me for this job was all that was needed, and I was hired.

From that day on, I became an employee of the German army *bekleidungs lager,* or clothing storage warehouse, at the AFL base. Along with about 40 or 50 other workers, I unloaded clothing supplies that came by train from German factories. We then sorted the uniforms, boots and helmets that were being transferred to other German army camps. After we sorted the clothing, we loaded it into boxes and put these onto trucks for further shipment. We worked from 8:00 in the morning until 5:00 in the afternoon, six days a week. Sunday was our day off. I traveled each morning from the ghetto to the AFL base on a special truck provided by the base. A special labor pass enabled me to leave and re-enter the ghetto.

As a bonus, every day the army provided us with a cooked lunch prepared in the base kitchens. We were served a thick soup containing rice, barley or potatoes. We could even receive more than one helping of this soup. We were provided with a German mess kit and a spoon. For the first time in many months, I was not hungry. I wished that I could take some of it home to my family.

The Germans liked me because I was energetic, efficient, and cheerful. We were paid for our work in German marks and I received, along with some others, a little extra money for my special efforts at work. With this, I was able to purchase from Polish civilian AFL employees, and smuggle into the ghetto, delicacies such as butter, sugar, cheese and a better-quality bread. This lifted everyone's spirits, and I felt proud that I was able to help support my family.

A smuggling network emerged at this camp. Many people contributed and cooperated in making the network a success. The network fed many Jews in the ghetto who otherwise would have starved.

Beautiful hand-knitted sweaters and shawls arrived from Germany for distribution to German soldiers on the Russian front. Those of us who worked in the clothing storerooms wore a different sweater out of the storeroom after work every evening. Because it was winter and we were still permitted to wear civilian clothes to work, the staff of the storeroom did not notice.

We sold these sweaters to Polish workers and took the money home on the weekends to our families. We were able to smuggle additional sweaters home by wearing them under our other clothes. Our family members in the ghetto wore them or sold them. This was an important supplement to our regular AFL salary.

Both Esther and I tried to convince my sister to get a job at the base as well. She refused. I pleaded with her, as did a couple of her other friends who also worked at the AFL, Edzia Rapaport and Pola Mandelbaum.

"Your friends Edzia and Pola sent their regards to you, Chaya," I would say to her. "They say that you are making a big mistake by refusing to come to work with us."

"Leave me alone. I don't want to go to work anywhere. Mind your own business, Lyzerke," she would say, starting to cry.

We argued often about her refusal to work. I wanted my sister to be protected with a labor pass as I was, and I felt she would be happier if she were not bored. But her steadfast negative attitude toward working frustrated me. I felt all she needed was a little confidence, and that I could help her gain that confidence. But I was unable to convince her that she could do the job. She was stubborn, and would not even try.

During spring 1942, a group of Russian prisoners

of war was brought onto the AFL base. The prisoners worked alongside us in the clothing storerooms. Chervony discovered that I was able to speak both German and Russian and occasionally asked me to translate his commands into Russian for the prisoners. Eventually, Chervony removed me from my regular job in the clothing storeroom and appointed me full-time translator. These prisoners came from the Tatar region, and many of them became my friends. They taught me their dialect and also some Tatar songs.

I was well known on the base for my singing. The Germans loved music and they asked me to sing for them often. I sang melodies in Polish, Yiddish, and German. The Germans gave me sweets or chocolate as a reward for singing. I put the candy in my pocket and smuggled it into the ghetto to share with Chaya.

That summer, the Germans decided that we should be permanent workers and live at the base. They constructed a special workers' camp for us, which contained barracks, latrines, and other facilities. We were ordered to sleep at the base during the week. On Saturday afternoon we were permitted to return to the ghetto so long as we were back by Monday morning. Workers who refused to comply with these new orders were fired immediately.

My parents and I decided that it would be best for me to comply with the orders and remain in the camp. I worried that I would miss my family during the week and that I would no longer be able to regularly supplement my family's food supply. But the idea of living at the camp made me feel independent, and this feeling overcame my initial reluctance to leave the ghetto. I knew, of course, that my family was there if I needed them.

The living conditions at the camp were comfortable, and the German employers from the *Wehrmacht* were not cruel. In fact, we developed a special "system" for dealing with the few instances when a German soldier became angry with one of us. The consequences were terrible because if a worker were fired, it meant he had to return to the ghetto without a labor pass. The "system" involved my friend, Esther Finkelshtein, whom the Germans called "Charna" because her hair was black. Esther was the camp "lawyer."

The German sergeant Chervony got his nickname because he had a bad temper. He would become red with rage if a worker was lazy or was caught lying or stealing. When this happened, word would quickly reach Esther. She had a talent for approaching Chervony.

She would talk to him and calm him down. We never heard the conversation, so we never knew exactly how she persuaded Chervony to change his mind. But when Esther intervened on a worker's behalf, the worker kept his or her job.

We were served one regular daily meal, plus bread, salami and cheese once a day. In addition, with the money we earned, we were able to purchase any additional food that we wanted. We slept on real mattresses with sheets that were washed regularly. In our leisure time, we played soccer with the Germans and with the Russian prisoners. Women workers were able to knit. We played cards, dominoes or other games.

One of the Jewish workers at the base, Mathis Vishnya, was a violinist from Radom. He had great big bushy eyebrows and long black hair parted on the right side. He also had big dark eyes that would close slowly as he played beautiful Jewish melodies. Almost every night, just after curfew, when we were already lying in our beds, Mathis took his violin from the black case which he kept under his bed, stood between two beds in the middle of the barrack, and, with a white handkerchief under his chin, began to play.

The barrack became silent as Mathis played sad melodies that reminded us of the world that used to be ours. He played ballads about thriving Jewish *shtetls* that existed no longer. I loved one such ballad in particular called "Darale." He played light classical music written by Jewish composers. My favorite melody was called "Rezignacia," a Jewish piece that calmed me, because it presented a peaceful vision of a world filled with kindness and hope. We all were grateful for this beautiful diversion in the evenings because our days were filled with uncertainties and fears about our families in the ghetto.

I looked forward to Saturdays, when I was permitted to go home. I missed my family and was anxious to bring them supplies that I had collected during the week. One Saturday, I was pleased to hear that Abush had been hired by the Pulka factory to work with my father. This job was an improvement over his last; not only did it pay more and allow him to work at home, but it also provided him with a valuable labor pass. Selections and deportations were occurring more frequently now, and unskilled ghetto residents were the targets.

On another of my weekends in the ghetto, I learned that Mayer, with whom I had shared the folded bed since I was a little boy, was in love and intended to get engaged. His fiancee's name was Pola. Pola was special. She had red hair that she wore in a ponytail, which bounced up and down behind her as she moved. She wore tiny pearl earrings, and always smiled. I thought Pola was beautiful, and I loved when she was in our home. I would stare at her, absolutely enchanted with her every move. Mayer began to spend more and more time with Pola and her family. And I got the bed all to myself!

For a short time, we had hope. All of the men in the family were working, and so we had a regular income. We were not hungry. We had labor passes to protect us from deportation. Mayer was in love. Things looked better. Maybe we could make it through this together.

PART THREE

A Cup of Honey

Early in July 1942, a rumor began to spread that all the inhabitants of the smaller Glinice ghetto were to be "resettled" in labor camps. Panic spread immediately, not just in the Glinice ghetto, but also in ours.

When I returned home from the AFL one weekend, I heard this rumor and, alarmed, I immediately asked my father about it. He was working.

"Papa, is it true that the Glinice ghetto is to be liquidated?"

Placing his leather and scissors down on the cutting table, my father looked at me and asked, "Where did you hear that, Lyzerke?"

"Everyone is talking about it, Papa. Surely you must have heard it, too," I replied.

I knew my father did not want to tell me what he knew. But I also could sense that he was terribly worried. His brother and sister-in-law and their family were in Glinice, having been taken there from a small town outside Radom. And he was worried for us because the rumor was that our ghetto would be next.

Frustrated that my father would not speak frankly with me, I turned to my mother. "Mama, please tell me what is going on."

My mother was preparing lunch. She stopped, dried her hands on her apron, and came over to me.

"Yes, we also have heard the rumors," my mother admitted, glancing now and then over at my father. "But I think we will be safe. You, your Papa, Abush and Mayer have work papers. The papers will protect us because the Germans need you. You are all professionals."

"So we do not want you to worry, Lyzerke," my father added. "You are safe at the AFL."

I wanted so badly for them to be with me, and I felt in my heart that the AFL was safer than the ghetto. I fantasized all the time that I would save my family and that we would be together again in a safe place. I was willing to do anything to make the fantasy become real.

"I can get a job for you, too. At the AFL. Even for you and Chaya, Mama," I pleaded.

My parents looked at each other and smiled when I said that. My mother knew that I thought as she did — always optimistically. But they knew that my plan was impossible. People from the ghetto were willing to pay thousands of zloty to secure a job at the AFL or another safe place. There simply were not enough spaces for all the people who wanted, so desperately, to be protected.

"We are secure at Pulka," my father assured me. "We do not need to leave there." But I did not believe him, and I remained deeply troubled.

On August 5, 1942, at midnight, an "action" started in the Glinice ghetto. By the next day, the entire ghetto was emptied and its former inhabitants, including my father's brother and his family, had disappeared. We heard that many people had tried to hide in special hiding places in the ghetto. When the SS discovered them, they were shot on the spot. Entire families — over 1,000 Jews had tried to escape deportation by hiding — were murdered in the streets of the Glinice ghetto and buried in a hastily-dug ditch in one of the ghetto's streets.

As we had predicted, the only people who were spared the deportation and the shootings were the skilled workers who possessed labor cards. These workers were relocated into our ghetto and it was from them that we learned about events that were almost too horrible to believe. We heard stories about SS men killing infants by smashing their heads against the walls of their own homes, and I did not believe it. I did not want to believe it. I could not sleep after this. I was horrified that my ghetto would be next.

Eleven days later it was. I came home as usual on Saturday afternoon and realized immediately what was happening. As I walked through the Shvarlikovska Street gate with Esther Finkelshtein, we could already feel the tension. Unable to sit still, everyone — old people, young people, men and women — wandered the streets like poisoned mice, looking frightened and worried. They were all trapped, and there was no escape.

We arrived home to find our families sitting together in the twilight waiting for the Sabbath to end. They rose when they heard us at the door. They were happy and relieved to see us.

"What is happening here?" Esther asked her parents as soon as we walked through the door. The mood in the room was somber, and the approaching darkness made it all the more threatening.

"It seems that this is the end of the ghetto," Esther's mother replied.

"How do you know this?" I asked.

"We have been hearing rumors for days that an "action" is near. When they heard the same rumors in the Glinice ghetto, it turned out to be true," Esther's mother reminded us.

I did not want to believe that she was right, so I looked over to my mother for reassurance. "Would you like a glass of hot tea?" my mother asked me in a warm voice.

"Yes, Mama, of course," I answered her. As my mother rose to get me the tea, Esther's family got up to return to their room.

"So, tell me what you have heard about the Glinice people, Mama," I suggested, to break the silence.

My mother began to boil the water in the kettle. "We have heard terrible news about the ghetto. The Jews were sent away." My mother looked down, overcome with grief.

"Where were they sent?" I asked quickly.

"Well, we don't know, and we have not heard news from anyone who was sent away," my mother said soothingly. Changing the subject, she added, "How was your week at the AFL?"

"Everything was fine. I brought you some things," I told her, pulling out some jam and canned sardines from my bag. My mother's face lit up when she saw what I had brought them.

"Chaya, let's make something to eat," she said.

I watched my mother and sister prepare supper and I felt sad. They moved around the little kitchen together in their usual coordinated way, and I realized how familiar the scene was to me. Mealtime in my home had always been the highlight of my day. I was happy just to sit there and watch them, and I almost forgot what was happening around us.

Our dinner that Saturday night consisted of my smuggled sardines and jam, along with some bread. We did not feel like eating anything at all but my mother, hoping to cheer us up, insisted that we sit at the table. During dinner, we decided that we should each prepare a small bag to grab in the event a similar "action" would occur in our ghetto. We knew that in Glinice, the SS had stormed into people's homes without giving them time to pack their belongings.

The following day, Sunday, August 16, was even more tense. We knew for certain that an "action" was imminent when we saw Polish electricians enter the ghetto and install giant spotlights on all the major street corners.

We saw other activities that were unusual for a Sunday. All day, we observed that members of the Jewish ghetto police were attending meetings with the SS in the *Judenrat* building and at the police station. They tried to assure us that nothing was going to happen, but we did not believe them. We sat around all afternoon waiting for information. Mayer and Pola came to our apartment around noon to spend some time with us but they brought no additional information.

Around 2:00 in the afternoon, Esther Finkelshtein came to me and said, "Lyzerke, I think that we should go back to the workers' camp earlier than usual this evening."

"Why?" I asked her.

"Don't you see what is happening outside?" she answered gently. "I hope they will let us out."

I did not respond and she left the room to pack.

After a minute or two, I announced to my parents that I had changed my mind and that I would not go back to the AFL at all, because I wanted to stay with them no matter what happened. I knew that my parents disagreed with me, but I did not want to be alone. I tried to find a way to convince them that I should stay. My arguments did not convince anyone. I decided to take a walk so I could think about what to do. I was confused, desperate, and already lonely.

When I got up, my mother followed. She caught up and said, "Come on, let's walk a little."

She led me to a corner of the backyard and put her hand on my shoulders.

"You know, Lyzerke, you risk losing your job at the AFL, if you remain here with us," she told me. I just stood there, silently, thinking about what my mother was saying.

"Look, my *tirenke,* my darling," she continued, "You are happier when you are working, and besides, you have responsibility there."

The sounds of the electricians and other workmen in the streets made me feel tense. My mother's words were soothing. She had a magical way of making the hurt fade away. She also knew how to convince me.

"Lyzerke, please understand one thing. We need you to keep working. The food and money you bring us keep us alive." After my mother said this, I knew I had no choice but to leave. My eyes filled with tears.

"Mama, I am afraid for you, for Papa, and for the family," I said in a low voice. "I don't want them to take you away," I cried, staring into the familiar big brown eyes.

"I am not afraid," she said, hugging me. "With God's will, everything will be all right."

We went back into the house. My mother silently began to pack a bag for me. She loaded extra socks, shirts, and underwear into the bag.

I watched her moving around, gathering my things, and I hoped she would change her mind. Chaya and Abush stood in the room watching her as well. They echoed my mother in trying to convince me that it would be best to return to the base before it was too late.

The afternoon passed quickly. We began to receive

alarming information from neighbors. A cordon of Ukrainian soldiers and SS surrounded the ghetto. In addition, the SS were placing machine guns on the roofs of the Polish houses outside the ghetto. Machine guns. Did they really think we were a physical threat to them? We had no weapons.

My mother began to urge me to leave. It was getting late. Esther and some other AFL workers had left long ago. At this point, we were not sure that even my special AFL worker pass would enable me to get past the checkpoint at the edge of the ghetto.

My mother lifted up my bag and softly said, "*Nu,* won't you say goodbye to your Papa and Abush?" My father and Abush stood to say goodbye to me. Mayer and Pola had already left for Pola's house and were not there to say goodbye. First I hugged my brother, then my father. I began to cry when I felt my father's arms protectively around me. My father kissed me.

Then he said, "Don't worry, everything will be all right."

I picked up my bag. My mother and Chaya followed me out the door. As I left the house, I kissed the *mezuzah* that was attached to the outside of our door. By this action, I asked the Almighty to watch me and to provide me with a safe journey.

As we stepped outside, I noticed that my mother was carrying in her hand a small white porcelain cup. The top was covered with paper, and she had secured it with string. My mother wrapped her right arm around my shoulder and carried the little cup in her left hand. Chaya walked on my right side. We proceeded slowly together up Shvarlikovska Street to the ghetto gate. I would have stopped the clock if I could have. I wanted time to slow so I could be close to them for a little longer.

As we walked, none of us knew what to say. To break the silence, I tried once again to argue with my mother.

"Mama," I said, "Maybe it would be best if I remain in the ghetto with you. No matter what happens, we should stay together, don't you agree?" My mother pleaded with me. For the first time, she admitted we might become separated. I will never forget her words, which she spoke like a benediction.

"Lyzerke, if there is anyone in the family with a chance to survive, it is you," she whispered. "Please do not miss this opportunity. I think it is *beshert*, meant to be."

By then we had reached the gate. There were other people, holding passes like mine, standing in line at the exit checkpoint. My mother turned to me and handed me the cup she had been carrying. She began to cry silently and hugged me tightly. She said, "Take this little cup with you. You will have a sweet life, my *tirenke.*"

She put the cup in my hand, and I moved the string and the paper to the side so that I could see inside. I was shocked. Of all things, the cup was full of honey. Who could find honey these days? I hadn't seen any in years.

"But..." I started to protest. They would need

food, even this, more than I. Then I saw in her eyes that my mother meant for me to have this cup of honey.

"I will, Mama," was my reply.

I reached for Chaya and gave her a final hug and she kissed me. I turned without a word and headed for the gate. I presented my pass to the Jewish policeman at the gate. I looked back at my mother and sister. By now, my mother was trying to smile and I knew that she wanted me to see her with a smile on her face. I turned, walked through the gate and out of the ghetto.

ᕕ

I made it past the checkpoint. My pass was still valid. When I reached the outside, I noticed there was a lot of activity. In the streets surrounding the ghetto were SS men and Ukrainian soldiers wearing battle helmets and holding guns. Some of the Ukrainians held leashes that secured the necks of growling German shepherd dogs.

I kept thinking of the deportation from the Glinice ghetto 11 days ago. I was terribly upset. It appeared as if the SS were indeed about to carry out the same brutal "action" here in my own ghetto and to my own family. The thought that my family was trapped inside this doomed ghetto was too horrible to grasp. I felt scared and helpless.

As soon as I started walking in the direction of the camp, I was stopped by a Ukrainian soldier. "Your pass," he demanded in German. I handed it to him, but before he could even glance at it, an SS officer approached. Grabbing my pass from the soldier's hand, the SS officer looked at it, and then at me. He compared the picture on the pass with my face and ordered me to open my bag.

While I held it open for him, the officer silently examined the contents of my bag. Then he saw the little cup of honey, which I was carrying in my hand.

"What is this?" he said, laughing at me.

I didn't answer. He took the cup away from me and held it in his fingers. He tore the paper off, put some of the honey on his finger and licked it.

"Honey. Hmmm. What are you going to do with this?" he said, still laughing like it was the funniest thing in the world.

I started to cry softly. The honey cup was still warm from my mother's fingers, and I did not want this awful man to touch it. It violated her somehow.

He then handed the cup back to me and ordered me to wait. He walked over to another officer. As nervous as I was, I hoped in my heart that the second officer would not approve my pass and would send me back to the ghetto.

The second SS officer called over to me.

"Where are you going?" he demanded in a suspicious voice.

I answered in German that I was on my way back to the AFL camp, at which I had been employed a long time as a professional. I told him that I was required to report for work very early in the morning.

He walked over to me and took my pass. After

examining it carefully, the officer forced me to remove my belongings from the bag. As I nervously, and perhaps too slowly, started to take out my things, the officer impatiently motioned me on my way. He said in German, *"Mach das schnell* (do it quickly)."

Numbly, I walked the three kilometers to the camp. All I could think about were my mother's words, repeating them in my mind over and over like a movie reel.

"If there is anyone in the family with a chance to survive, it is you," she had said. "Have a sweet life, my *tirenke."*

On the way, I met others who were returning to the base. Their faces looked the way I felt: petrified and confused. When we arrived, we walked straight to our barracks.

It was still light outside. We spent hours recounting our stories about the terrible events of that day in the ghetto. Some of us tried to calm ourselves and our friends. Others were more realistic and argued that we should not fool ourselves, that our ghetto was about to suffer the same fate as Glinice.

Although we were exhausted, none of us felt like sleeping. As night fell, we finally turned out the lights. I lay down in my bed and the base suddenly became eerily quiet. There was no sound in my barrack or from any other. We retreated into a trance-like state, immersed in our memories of the final moments we had spent with our families.

I was lonely. I tried softly to speak with my

friends, Heniek and Yezyk Rosenberg, brothers from Radom who were about my age, but they had already fallen asleep. I reached for the cup of honey, and held it tightly in my hands. I finally fell into a light sleep.

Shortly after midnight, we awoke to the distant but horrifying sound of machine-gun fire. We were forbidden to leave the barrack, but in my mind, I was in the ghetto with my parents. I could not stop imagining where my mother was at any given moment. I could see her standing in line, then being pushed or dragged into a waiting train. In my imagination, my mother was not smiling, but was terribly frightened.

I could also imagine other mothers with young children, crying as they were shoved and pushed about in the confusion. I could see in my mind the panic in the tearful faces of the young children as they were separated from their mothers. I could hear the growling and loud barking of the German dogs as they were commanded to attack those who were not moving through the streets quickly enough. I could hear these things even though I was not there, and I felt terribly helpless.

Somehow, dawn reached Radom the next day. I was finally allowed to leave the barrack. I looked toward the train tracks that led from the Maryvil railroad station. What I saw haunts me to this day.

On the tracks stretched a long line of sealed, dark-brown freight trains. Walking or running alongside the trains were dozens of SS men accompanied by fierce dogs, Ukrainian soldiers, and even Jewish ghetto police. I saw piles of suitcases and bundles of personal belongings in different colors, lying alongside the trains, apparently discarded in the haste and confusion. I heard the sound of gunfire mingled with the shouting of loud, angry commands in a language that I could not make out.

The workday began and we had to report to our posts. Somehow, the sun rose high in the sky and blanketed the sad place with light and heat. Suddenly, a message came to us that the SS had arrived and were searching the base for anyone under the age of 16. I had just turned 14 in July, but in the base records, I was registered as 16, so I was not too worried about being taken away.

My friend Yezyk Rosenberg, however, was registered as a 15-year-old, so I was worried about him. I found out later that his older brother succeeded in hiding him in the camp. The *Wehrmacht* soldiers who ran the camp apparently knew about this attempt to hide Yezyk but to our amazement, did not make any effort to aid the SS men's angry and frantic search. To me, it is a miracle that none of the many children who were working in the base were turned over to the SS for deportation.

The trains sat still all through the morning. The sun became hotter and more intense. It must have been unbearably hot and stuffy in those crowded, airless wagons. We prayed the entire morning that the trains would not leave, that the people would come out of the trains and that they would return to the ghetto.

But finally the trains slowly began to pull out from the station. Word of the departure traveled quickly throughout the base and we ran to have a view. We stood in silence for the three minutes or so that it took the trains to disappear. Even the German *Wehrmacht* soldiers watched the trains leaving. When the trains had gone, we all turned around and, with heavy hearts, returned to work.

At our lunch break we spoke about the only topic on our minds. Where had the trains gone? Rumors spread quickly. One was that the trains had taken our families to some unknown labor camp for "resettlement." Another was that the trains had gone to the Russian border. Whatever we heard calmed us because we wanted so badly to hear news that was not terrible. Rumors of extermination camps spread but we discounted them because we did not want to believe that our families were already on their way to their deaths. We had never heard the name "Treblinka."

PART FOUR

Like a Dream You Vanished

For an entire week, we tried to obtain information about our families. We heard that some skilled workers remained in the ghetto. I knew that Abush, Mayer, and my father were considered skilled workers, and I hoped in my heart that I would find them again.

We devised a plan to return to the ghetto. Some workers asked the German camp commander if we could return to collect some personal items. They explained to the Germans that, in our haste to leave the ghetto, we had not brought enough clothes with us from our homes. The soldiers agreed to take us by truck to the ghetto the next Sunday, August 24.

On Sunday morning a truck arrived. Hans, a German driver with a limp, drove us to the ghetto and told us we had a few hours to collect our belongings and that we should meet at 4:00 that afternoon to return to the camp.

We were shocked by what we saw. The streets were almost deserted, like a ghost town. It was a mess —

scattered all over the cobblestones were suitcases and other bundles, some still closed but others open with their contents strewn about — clothing, shoes, children's toys. There were empty baby carriages, many lying on their sides. Someone had begun to clean the streets, and there were huge piles of debris everywhere. I was anxious but hopeful.

Survivors of the deportation began to appear from nowhere, like ghosts. They continued to emerge as we walked through Spitalna Street to Shvarlikovska Street. They looked traumatized. It had been one week since the deportation and they still wore expressions of horror. As they saw us approaching, they ran over to us.

"Where did you come from?" someone said. We all were hoping to find a relative among the ruins of our families' ghetto homes.

I remember feeling jealous as I witnessed one such reunion. Edzia Rapaport, an AFL worker who I knew well because she was a close friend of Chaya's, found a cousin in the street. They held each other for several minutes, sobbing. I wanted so badly to meet someone from my family.

I heard my nickname shouted in the distance. "Lyzerke!" As I turned around, I saw a family friend, Zalmy. He cried to me, "Your brother, Abush, is in the ghetto. I saw him today!"

I stopped, shocked. "Yes? Where is he?" I yelled. But I did not even listen for his answer. I ran as fast as I could in the direction of our ghetto home at Shvarlikovska 26.

As I approached I could see through the window at least two figures sitting in our room. Could it be my beloved brother, Abush? My father? By some miracle, my beautiful mother? Were they waiting for me to return to them? I carried some food with me, hoping that I would find and share it with a member of my family.

I think I flew up the stairs, around the corner and through the small courtyard into the doorway of my home. I must have flown because I do not remember that my feet touched the ground. As I entered the doorway, I noticed with alarm that the place was in disarray. The glass on the dish cupboard was broken. Dishes and clothes were strewn all around. Then I saw my father standing there with his arms outstretched. He must have seen me approaching the house through the low window. He had been sitting there for days hoping I would return. He was with a friend who also had survived the deportation.

My father was unshaven, his clothes had not been changed for a long time — perhaps since the deportation — and his eyes were red. As he grabbed me, we both cried for several minutes and I remember trying to look into his eyes to find information about my mother and the rest of my family, but he would not look at me. That was how I knew what had happened to my mother, my sister Chaya, and my brother Mayer.

He told me that he and my brother Abush had just heard that the AFL workers had returned. Abush had gone to the gate to find me. I could tell that my father had not eaten in days, and I offered him the food that I had brought with me. He refused it. Then he told me the story of the deportation.

After my mother and Chaya walked me to the gate that terrible afternoon, they returned home. By that time people had started running through the streets in panic. The SS were spreading false rumors that there would be no deportation. But these rumors conflicted with other, more realistic signs, such as heavily increased armed patrols.

By 8:00 that evening, the ghetto gates were sealed and it became impossible for anyone to leave, even with a worker pass like mine. After 8:00, messages began to spread that people should pack in preparation for travel. The instructions were that a two-day supply of food should be packed and that any personal jewelry should also be included.

At midnight, after spending a final, terrifying evening at home together, my family began to hear loud commands shouted in the streets. SS soldiers, Ukrainian soldiers, and Jewish ghetto police were shouting instructions from the streets that the people should assemble imme-diately in Stare-Miastro (Old City) Square with their food and jewelry.

"Hurry up!" they shouted. "You must go quickly to Rynek Square!"

My family decided to comply with these commands and began to walk together down the cobblestones toward the square.

My father told me that he tried, above all else, to stay together with my mother and the rest of the family. As they continued on their way, however, it became harder to keep together because many thousands of people, whole families, including parents with small children, were also streaming into the center of the ghetto.

As my family arrived in the square, they saw almost the entire ghetto population already assembled. It was apparent that the events in the Glinice ghetto were being repeated. The Germans first divided people into two groups. Older people, women with children, and men and women without work documents were ordered to assemble on one side of the square, and men and women with work papers were instructed immediately to move to another side. The Germans shouted and screamed at people to hurry. The selection was all over in seconds. And my father lost my mother and Chaya.

"I tried to stay together with them." He was trembling. "And I thought your mother and sister were with me. But all of a sudden I felt strong blows on my back and side. I turned toward the Ukrainian soldier who was beating me, and I tried to show him my work pass, but all I could think about was your mother and Chaya. But they were gone. I was not able to say goodbye to them. The next thing I knew, Abush was showing an SS soldier our work passes, and we were approved for work detail.

"Did you see Mama and Chaya again? Where did they go?" I wanted so desperately to know.

"Abush and I looked all over the square for them. We never saw them again." My father put his head in his hands and sobbed.

I started to cry and reached for my father. After a

few minutes, I said: "Did you see Mayer? What happened to Pola and Mayer?"

"I did not see him or Pola at all. But I am sure that Mayer went with Pola and did not show his pass."

As I was listening to my father describe these horrifying events, I could not remove my mother's face from my mind. I imagined her as she moved through the deportation lines. I knew that she had a realistic notion of what would be her fate. I also knew that she wanted, more than anything, for the rest of us to be safe and felt relieved that my father, Abush, and I had a chance to survive the deportation.

I was becoming impatient to see Abush. I kept glancing restlessly through the window. Finally, the familiar figure of my brother appeared and I jumped up to greet him. We held each other tightly.

I asked him the question that was uppermost in my mind: "Where did they go, Abush?"

He told me what would take me months to believe. "It lasted two or three days," he said softly. "Twenty thousand Jews were taken away. We hear rumors that they went to a place called Treblinka. You know they went in trains. But they were not passenger trains. They were for animals. I do not think we will see them again."

He continued to speak softly. I was afraid he was going to upset my father the way he was talking. I could tell that my father still thought my mother would return.

"Only about 5,000 ghetto residents are still here," Abush continued. "All of us are registered as skilled workers. I think we will be safe now."

"I want you both to come with me," I demanded. "I will get you a job at my base. You will be safe there. You cannot remain in this place. They will take you away."

"We are protected as well," my brother said. They need us to work at Pulka." He glanced over at my father's white face. "Plus, Daddy wants to be here when Mama returns."

I left soon after that. I was sure I would see them soon, and I promised to come as often as I could. When I met the other AFL workers that afternoon, we shared our experiences. Most people had found no surviving family members. In their former homes, they found possessions only. Most homes looked as if people had left in a hurried panic, as if an earthquake had struck. One person found a cup of tea still on the table, not yet drunk, along with a piece of bread that was now dry.

Two of my friends from the clothing storehouse, brothers Nortan and Moshe Himelfarb, asked me and Yezyk and Heniek Rosenberg to follow them into their family's deserted apartment and *galanteria,* or notions shop. They told us to take any items we might need. They would rather we took them than bear the thought of the Germans or Poles using their family's treasured things.

The Himelfarbs allowed me to take a dark gray winter jacket with a fur collar. This jacket was to become valuable when the weather became bitter cold later that year. Eventually, though, I felt uncomfortable wearing the jacket because I knew that the Himelfarbs, although they would never admit it, would love to have it back. I decided to return the jacket. I approached Moshe Himelfarb in our barrack. "You know, Moshe, I appreciate that you let me use the jacket," I began, "but it is too small through the shoulders. I'd like to give it back."

Looking at me with surprise, Moshe started to protest, "But we gave it to you, and besides, it is bitter cold outside. What will you wear?" he said to me.

"I'll be all right," I lied. "I will take a jacket from the storeroom. I will manage."

Moshe looked grateful as he reluctantly took back the jacket. I felt cold, but happy that I had in a small way been able to return to him a piece of his past.

èa

As we left the ghetto that first Sunday after the deportation, I had mixed feelings. I felt lucky that, unlike most other workers, I still had a father and brother in the ghetto. Many of my friends had no one left. On the other hand, I missed my dear mother and the rest of my family terribly. I felt emotionally exhausted.

The weeks dragged on. Residents of the ghetto faced continuing daily threats. Without warning, the SS would take innocent individuals from the ghetto and ship them away. I realized that my father and brother might disappear the same way. So I secured them each a job at the AFL base and I arranged that they could live with me in the barracks. To my frustration and dismay, however, my father and Abush still would not agree to leave the ghetto.

Neither of them wanted to live in what had become a "camp." They preferred instead to stay home in our now roomy ghetto apartment. They felt that a better strategy for what was left of our family was to remain separated. If anything happened to them, at least I might be safe. Or, if any of us needed help, there was the possibility that the others could provide it. We remained separated.

During the fall and the beginning of the winter of 1942, I had only sporadic contact with my father and Abush. We were able to get messages to each other, but I was not permitted to return home at all. I learned frightful things about what was happening to the remaining ghetto residents.

People were being captured, tortured, and shot in front of their neighbors, not as punishment for any particular offense, but to establish an atmosphere of fear. The Nazis wanted us to understand that they controlled our lives. These raids happened constantly and, one by one, people disappeared. I slept very little, worrying that a similar raid might take my father or Abush.

By the beginning of December 1942, I was anguished by my lack of contact with my family. One day, as I was working in the storehouse, a train entered the ramp loaded with clothing, boots, and equipment. My group was mobilized to unload the boots and to deliver them to our storehouse. It was late, and it had begun to rain. As I was carrying a huge load of boots on my shoulders, I slipped on the wet ramp. Before I knew what was happening, I landed on the hard, wet ground four or five feet below. I felt excruciating pains shoot up my leg and started to scream.

My friends ran over to me. When they saw my left leg twisted in two different directions, it was obvious what had happened. Hearing the commotion, the German sergeant Chervony rushed over to me and ordered my friends to place me on his shoulders. He carried me to my barrack, and, with a knife, removed my shoe from my swollen foot.

The Germans next made arrangements to transfer me to the ghetto hospital. Chervony, along with the driver, Hans, came to take me to the truck. When they arrived, they realized that I was in pain so they fetched a stretcher as well as pieces of wood. With the wood and some string, they created a makeshift splint and carried me on the stretcher to the truck. The next thing I knew, I was delivered, on the stretcher, to the ghetto gate. Hans, the driver, turned me over to the Jewish Ghetto Police, but stayed with me.

Two Jewish policemen carried me on the stretcher from the gate to the hospital. I was apprehensive. I knew that it was dangerous to be in the ghetto without a job. With a broken leg, of course, I could not work. I faced the real danger of roundup and deportation.

But I also was eager to have regular contact with my father and brother again. Now that I would be in the hospital, they could visit me. Confused, I began to cry. Hans, who walked alongside my stretcher as I was being taken to the hospital, waited as the doctor diagnosed my problem as a fractured leg. Hans then whispered to me. "Hershenfis," he said, "don't worry, you will be all right." Then he added, "And you will come back to work at the AFL." I felt better.

After I arrived at the hospital, I discovered an eerie coincidence. "*Beshert!*" My hospital was located less than one block from my ghetto home, just behind Shvarlikovska Street. I asked one of the hospital workers to fetch my father or brother.

My father arrived a few minutes later, worried but happy to see me. The next three and a half weeks presented a bittersweet opportunity. My leg was set and fixed, but without anesthesia. It hurt like no other hurt I had ever experienced. But it was worth it in a way. I was able to see my father and Abush every day for three weeks. Each day, my father brought me soup that he had made from potatoes, rice, and beans.

But hospital patients were in constant danger. On New Year's Eve I was lying in my hospital bed in a small room that I shared with five other patients. Opposite me lay a man my brother's age who worked in a metal-working factory. His name was Yitzchak but we called him *"Itche mit de kily,"* or "Itche with the hernia." He used to amuse us with jokes, funny faces, and Yiddish songs. His favorite song was about a little Jewish boy who was warned gently not to tell the secrets from the *cheder*, the religious school.

We were worried. The Germans celebrated their "Sylvester Night" on December 31 and were known to become drunk and dangerous. As we lay sleeping after midnight, we were awakened by the sound of frightening screams in the direction of the hospital entrance just down the corridor from our room. The languages were German and Polish, although we could not make out the words.

We heard doors slamming, muffled arguing, and, finally, gunshots. We also heard German drinking songs, which further fed our fears. We sat up in our beds bracing ourselves for whatever might happen. After a long 10 minutes, the silence returned and we lay completely still — glued to our beds—hoping the brawlers would not return.

Early the next morning, New Year's Day 1943, we again heard noises in the corridors, but this time there was only loud talking. The nurse came into our room and told us that the previous evening, the Germans had entered the hospital with a list of Jews to kill. The targets were Jewish doctors and other prominent people. The Germans sought young Jewish nurses and raped them. They murdered five Jews that night, including at least one of the doctors at the hospital. A prominent member of the *Judenrat* was taken away. My brother reported to me that everyone in the ghetto was talking about these murders, but that this kind of activity was becoming so commonplace that they had stopped wondering whether there would be another tragedy, and just wondered who would be next. My brother also told me that he had begun to sleep in the attic to avoid being rounded up for deportation.

I heard reports that eased my constant fear of being deported. The messages were that the Chervony wanted me back and that I would be taken to the AFL when I recovered. Yet my leg did not heal quickly, and although my cast was finally removed, I was still limping and in pain.

I was released from the hospital and went home to continue recuperating. I knew if I returned to the base, I would not be able to work. My leg hurt too badly for me to stand for long.

Edzia Rapaport, whom I had seen the day we returned to the ghetto after the deportation, in a happy reunion with a cousin, had lost all her immediate family. Edzia was my favorite among Chaya's friends. She had a beautiful singing voice and used to sing for us at the AFL.

Amidst all the destruction and sadness around us, Edzia fell in love with a boy named Tepper, also an AFL worker. They decided to get married. The authorities at the AFL agreed to allow the young couple to return to the ghetto for one night so that they could be married. Of course, there was no place at the AFL base for a couple to be together. So while I was home with a sore leg, Esther Finkelshtein offered the couple her room in my house for their first night together. I felt sad that my sister, Chaya, did not see her friend begin her marriage in our own home.

When Edzia arrived with her new husband, she could sense my worry that my disability would prevent me from working again. She assured me that she would speak with Chervony and would arrange some light work for me to do until my leg healed.

A few days later, rumors penetrated the ghetto that another "action" was being planned. My brother

Abush decided that I should return immediately to the AFL base. This time, we did not argue or even discuss the matter because I knew that I must secure my working place and that I had no chance to survive the deportation without a job.

Abush quickly arranged transportation for me to return to the AFL. He hired a *doroshka,* a horse-drawn carriage, to meet me at the ghetto gate. I packed some of my things, including pictures of my family and my small prayerbook. I dressed in my green AFL workclothes. My brother borrowed 300 zloty from me and promised to return it soon.

I hugged my father tightly.

"Take care of yourself, Lyzerke," my father said to me. "Be careful with your leg."

"I will see you soon. I will come back home," I replied. He began to cry.

I turned to Abush. "Are you ready?"

"Yes, I am," he answered. He picked up my bag and we left home slowly. I was not worried. I expected to see them soon.

Late in the day, January 13, 1943, information arrived at the AFL. We found out that early that same morning, the SS had burst into the ghetto and ordered every Jew to gather immediately at Shvarlikovska 24, an empty courtyard next door to my ghetto house. The ghetto was surrounded by guards with machine guns. Anyone found hiding or trying to escape was shot by the SS or by the Ukrainian guards.

Children of families who had survived the earlier deportations were torn from their parents' arms, and infants were thrown in the air and shot by the commander of the "action" himself, an SS man named Schippers. Other small children were thrown against the walls of the ghetto houses, their skulls crushed in front of their parents' eyes.

My father and Abush were not protected by their labor cards this time. They were herded along with almost 2,000 people under heavy guard to the railway station and shipped away. A few Jews remained after the deportation, but for me, the ghetto was finished. I knew that I was alone.

PART FIVE

Nightmare

The next summer, we realized that our months of "protection" by the AFL authorities also must end. Orders from Gestapo headquarters were to deport all Jewish workers to other camps for forced labor. We heard rumors about possible destinations. We heard names of places like Majdanek, Blizyn, Plaszow and others. I was scared because I knew these names well. They were known to be concentration camps guarded by dreaded and brutal Ukrainian soldiers.

Some time in August, 1943, we were called together for a meeting in a storeroom of the clothing department. The German camp commander appeared. He told us that he had received orders we must be transferred to a labor camp in Poland called Blizyn. He said we were needed there because we were professionals. We were to leave the next morning at 9:00.

That afternoon was sad for all Jewish AFL workers. Some people planned to escape the deportation and to re-enter the ghetto which, by now, had become a forced labor camp. My friends, Yezyk and Heniek Rosenberg, who were blond and looked like Poles, succeeded in making the escape to the ghetto but I knew that I stood little chance of making it. My leg was not fully healed. I still limped and could not move quickly.

That evening we said goodbye to the Tatars and to our Polish co-workers. They were unhappy to see us leave. We had become friends. One of my Tatar friends told me not to forget the songs they had taught us. The words to these songs expressed my own feelings well — they reflected our longing to return home. I cried as I said goodbye to them. *"Dosvidanya,"* I said to them, "see you again."

The following day, open trucks appeared in front of our barracks driven by Ukrainian drivers wearing black uniforms. The Tatar prisoners, together with our Polish friends, were already preparing to replace us at our jobs. We were ordered to climb onto the trucks with our belongings. The Ukrainian guards actually helped us board. We took with us some bread and cheese, and even some butter. I carefully placed my butter into the honey cup that my mother had given me.

We were counted by the AFL authorities and recounted by the Ukrainians. They called each of our names. We knew that we were to enter a new world and our lives would never be the same. I saw Chervony and Hans and other Germans who had been our supervisors. They had sad faces. We could hear them saying *"Aufwiedersehen."*

As we left the AFL gates, we looked back at the familiar base and already longed to return. As we passed the city of Radom I wondered if I would ever see it again. I had a feeling I would not return to my home. So I tried to remember every detail of the place — the cobblestone streets, the entrance to the AFL base, the ghetto. After driving about an hour and a half, we arrived at a small village surrounded by thick forest. The sign at the entrance to the village said: "Blizyn."

❧

I discovered later that this camp was a satellite to the larger and more notorious camp, Majdanek, located near Lublin, Poland. My first impression was that I could never survive such a place.

I saw guard towers looming over the gray buildings, and barbed wire surrounding the forested compound. There were strange-looking, dirty people standing inside dressed in oversized clothes. Their eyes were hollow and they did not smile. They wore wooden clogs on their feet. They also wore, as part of their clothing, a belt or string to which was attached a tin bowl and spoon.

I became depressed. I could not imagine myself looking like these poor inmates. I tried to think of a way to avoid their fate. It would be different for me. I would not let this happen to me.

As soon as the truck stopped in an entrance courtyard, the same Ukrainian guards who were helpful to us when we were leaving the AFL became brutal. They pushed us off the trucks with their rifle butts and ordered us to move to a corner of the courtyard. There we began to see inmates walking toward us whom we knew from Radom. They had heard that we had arrived and found some excuse to take a walk in our direction. Everyone was eager to find someone they knew from home or any thread of information about family or friends.

I saw some people I recognized. They tried to give me valuable information. Someone told me in Hebrew and Yiddish: *"Bahalt die kesef,"* or "hide the money." I had already sewed the 800 or so zloty that I owned into the rim of my hat.

The Ukrainians began to push us in the direction of the camp's *Appelplatz,* or roll call field. The guards kept yelling and screaming, *"Schnell, Schnell!*—Hurry up, Hurry up!" Anyone who stumbled or who did not run quickly enough was kicked or beaten with a rifle butt.

The Ukrainian guards soon were joined by SS guards and by Jewish *kapos,* members of an internal police force set up by the SS. I was amazed to see how cruel these *kapos* were. I expected the Nazis to hate us and even the Ukrainians' cruelty did not surprise me. But these *kapos* were from our towns and once walked together with us in our streets. They were dressed in civilian clothes and wore high black boots with whips secured inside. Rewarded for their cruelty, they received plenty of food as well as warm, adequate clothing. They were recognized by their navy arm band, with the word *"Kapo"* in red letters.

When we arrived, out of breath, at the *Appelplatz,* we were ordered to place all our belongings on the ground and to open our bags for inspection. We were forced to throw out onto the ground the contents of our bags. I felt that I was being stripped of the last remaining remnants of my former life. While the guards were not looking, I placed gently all of my things, including my family photographs, onto the ground. But I could not bear to part with my small honey cup. I held it in my hand and curled my fingers around it.

An SS officer approached me with a stick, saw the cup, and slapped my hand to force me to release it. The cup fell to the ground, and broke into many pieces. The blow from the stick stung, but my eyes watered for the honey cup and not from the pain. Then the guard pushed all of our personal items into one great big pile on the side.

We reported to the Jewish block clerk, or *Blockschreiber,* our names, date and place of birth, and from where we came. We also reported to the clerk our profession. I told him that I knew how to repair shoes. Then we were given a dirty tin bowl with a spoon and ordered to stand and wait. After we were registered, a *kapo* appeared with the German camp commander. The *kapo* then welcomed us to the camp.

In Polish, we were told that we had arrived at the labor camp Blizyn, and that those who attempted to escape or even to approach the electrified fences surrounding the camp would be shot immediately and without warning. We were forbidden to have any contact with outsiders. Money was not allowed to be kept or used in the camp. We must appear at the roll call, or *Appel,* in the morning and in the evening exactly on time. If we did not appear on time for food distribution, we would not receive any food. We would work in a workshop according to our profession. We must obey the orders of the *kapos* and the *Blockaltester,* or block senior. We were warned that we would be shot if we walked outside the barrack after the curfew. If the guards were to discover any sabotage in the camp, the perpetrator would be found and immediately shot.

This was the first time under the Nazis that I felt completely powerless. My survival depended now on the whims of cruel, brutal strangers who took pleasure in my suffering. I had come from a protected life. I was the *mezunek* and was well-protected by my parents and siblings. At the AFL camp, even the Germans liked me and treated me fairly well. Now, I was in this strange, cold place where my every action was regulated and where any small deviation from the regulations meant torture or death.

Assigned to a barrack, I set off immediately for it. I was exhausted and very hungry. We had been in our new "home" for almost 10 hours and had not eaten anything all day except for the small amount of food we took with us from the AFL. We had been standing since we had arrived at the camp, without any chance to rest. My left leg ached.

I arrived at Barrack 20, the workshops barrack. This was a long wooden hut containing two-tiered wooden bunk beds with thin straw mattresses on which we were assigned a place to sleep. I could not believe my eyes. I had slept in cramped quarters all my life, but this was different. We were supposed to spend the night on boards?

There were no bathrooms in the barracks. We were to use the latrine, which was at least 150 or 200 yards from the barrack. The latrine consisted of a doorless wooden shack with holes in the wooden floor. There was always powdered chlorine on the floor, which we had to walk through to get to the holes. There was no paper. In the morning we waited in long lines to reach this building, and those who were unable to wait were beaten brutally. I tried always to be among the first to reach the latrine in the morning.

At night, after curfew, our barrack door was locked and we were not allowed to go to the latrine. Instead, we were supposed to use a container placed in the center of our barrack in full view of everyone. In the morning, this container was overflowing and the stench was horrible.

I had always thought the Germans were civilized people. How could they have set up these camps with the most inhumane conditions conceivable? Everything seemed calculated to make us feel like animals, not like people.

The food rations in this camp also made us feel like animals. The Germans fed their dogs much better than they fed us. The rations consisted of a quarter ladle of chicory-flavored water at 5:30 in the morning for breakfast; a watery soup that contained an occasional piece of potato peel for lunch; once a week a small slice of sausage or some jam; and for the evening "meal" a small portion of black bread. The bread was distributed to us in groups. We were supposed to divide one loaf among six people. We became so hungry on this inadequate diet that we devised a means to apportion the bread so we all received exactly the same amount. Every crumb was critical.

My group appointed a man named Chilek as the divider. We invented a primitive scale that someone built in his workshop out of wood, cardboard, and string. As Chilek would cut each division, the two pieces were weighed and any shortage was equalized. Then the division continued until six equal pieces were placed on Chilek's bed. None of us wanted the ends of the loaf, even though they weighed exactly the same as the other portions. Somehow, the ends seemed smaller.

Chilek had cut from cardboard a set of numbers. He would place a number on each portion of bread and would place an identical set of numbers in a hat. Everyone in the group would draw a number from the hat and then would grab hungrily his corresponding portion. Sometimes I would draw a number that corresponded with the end portion and other times not.

We liked this system because it was the fairest way to apportion our most precious and valuable treasure. It was amazing that we were able to wait for the weighing each evening. After a full day of labor and almost no food, we were starving. I would have given up anything for a full loaf of bread, and yet I had to wait while one was divided six ways.

I realized how civilized this procedure was, especially under the circumstances. The Nazis tried to reduce our living conditions to worse than those of animals, and yet, here we were, thinking, reasoning humans devising ways to create fairness. No starving animal would have done that.

The lunchtime soup was distributed outdoors no matter what the weather. In the rain or in the snow, we stood in line each day. A tall, handsome young inmate named Chaim stood with a large barrel of soup near the camp kitchen. Chaim was accompanied by an SS guard and a *kapo* who held a wooden baton in his hand. They both watched the soup line carefully, ready to beat anyone who might enter the line more than once or who might be given more than one ladle of soup.

We carefully watched Chaim's hand as he ladled our portion. I tried to hold my tin bowl perfectly in place so that not a single drop of the watery liquid would fall into or outside the barrel instead of into my bowl. I felt lucky if my turn came when the soup barrel was almost empty. I prayed to reach the ladle at this point because the soup might contain a little potato peel.

I knew Chaim from the AFL base. Occasionally, he would give me a small scoop extra if no one was watching. I was weak and starving and was willing to risk a beating to receive a small portion extra. I cannot explain why Chaim was willing to take a risk for me.

Sometimes it was possible to sneak back into the line at the end to receive seconds. If I stood near the barrel, I would be in a better position not only to see whether there was any food left at the bottom of the barrel, but also to be among the first to run into the line a second time if there was. We all adopted this strategy so that as we ate our soup, our eyes were not looking down at our food but rather were darting all around as we weighed our possible options to receive more.

After I had been in the camp for three months, in November, 1943, I was weak, hungry, and freezing. Impatiently I waited for the moment to arrive when I would receive my next portion of watery soup. Next to Chaim stood a tall, strong *kapo* who I knew from Radom. He had prayed next to my father in our synagogue and he had been fond of me. Every time he saw me in synagogue, he used to pinch my cheek.

When I saw him standing next to the soup barrel, I tried to catch his eye but he ignored me. As usual, my eyes were glued to the end of the line and I noticed that after everyone had gone through the line, there was some food remaining in the barrel. I ran back to the line, together with many others, hoping to obtain a small portion of additional food. On this day, everyone was pushing to reach the barrel first. I was pushed out by stronger men, but I tried to secure a place in the line.

Just then, to my shock, the *kapo* I knew grabbed me, and with his baton, began to beat me on the back. I tried to get away from him but he pursued me like a madman. I covered my face with my hands but he beat me on my hands. I was crying and screaming in pain, but he would not stop beating me. My tin bowl fell down on the ground and I panicked in fear it would be stolen, so I dove after the bowl and ran away.

I was in so much pain after the beating that I could not sleep at night for a week. I continued crying, not because of the pain, but rather because I felt hurt, humiliated, and abandoned. This man had prayed next to my family in the synagogue, and knew me well. He was not hungry. I merely was trying to obtain a little more food. Before the beating, I had looked into this man's eyes searching for understanding or even for some affection. And he responded by beating me all over my body.

I worked every day in a shoemaking workshop not far from my barrack. I sat in the middle of the room in a row of low tables and I was required, like everyone else, to produce a daily quota of the wooden clogs that the Germans provided to Russian war prisoners at Majdanek. Our job was to hammer nails through leather strips and into pieces of flat wood. Then we would write our assigned number on the bottom of each clog as a signature. Our work quantity and quality were constantly monitored. Only good and productive workers remained in this workshop.

I learned the technique of making these simple clogs on my first day on the job. Chaim Tepperman, my brother's friend from Radom who was one of the few of us who really was a shoemaker, taught me how to nail the strips to the wooden sole. Over time, I became an expert at this task. The director of the workshop used to present my work as a model to the German inspector.

Winter 1943 quickly smothered Blizyn, and presented special problems, especially during the twice-daily roll calls. At 5:30 in the morning, we were awakened by the sound of screaming and yelling. We were expected to jump immediately out of the bunks, run quickly to the latrine, and be ready on time to assemble in the *Appelplatz* block by block. We had to repeat this procedure in the evening after work. We stood outside, sometimes for hours, while the block senior, along with the German block inspector, counted us. In the event anyone was missing, we would wait for hours longer until the person was found.

We stood outside like that even in the rain or snow, and it did not matter whether there were blizzards or strong winds. I had a thin jacket only, and within seconds my body became numb. The only thing I could do to prevent frostbite was to stomp my feet. I saw weaker inmates collapse on the ground. We were not allowed to help a fallen inmate. He remained there, lying in the snow. Dismissal from these events brought enormous relief just to be able to go inside to thaw fingers and toes.

One cold winter morning, after we had endured a few days of roll calls in the constant snow, there was about 15 inches of snow on the ground. I was hurrying to the latrine before the *Appel*, hoping to make it before a line started forming. I did not want to wait outside the latrine in the bitter weather. It was still dark outside and I could not see well. All of a sudden, I saw out of the corner of my eye the figure of an armed SS guard. Before I could even think, I heard a loud order, "Halt!"

I stopped immediately and looked towards the guard, who was approaching me. He was angry and moved fast.

"Why did you not remove your hat when you saw me?" he demanded.

"I didn't see you," I replied.

Furious, he pushed me into the cold, wet snow face-down. I was scared to death. We were alone in the darkness and I knew it would not be out of the ordinary for him simply to shoot me. He ordered me to get up and then he continued to push me down into the snow with his boot. Each time he pushed me down, he would then order me to stand up. This continued at least 10 times. Each time I would drag my body out of the snow to my feet. Finally, he let me go. I ran, wet and cold, back to my barrack, having lost the need to go to the latrine.

I was relieved that I was permitted to get away alive. But I was angry. I had not been punished before by a Nazi guard, and it seemed to me that the punishment I suffered amused him just as much as it hurt me. He was cold and barbaric.

I was trying hard to follow their crazy rules and, yet, that did not matter here. One of the cruelest realities was that in this place, my fate did not depend on how well I followed rules or performed my duties. Instead, my life depended on instant whims of these guards, who were thrilled to humiliate and torture victims like me for no reason at all.

That winter I also lost one of my most valuable possessions — my leather shoes. One morning I woke up to find that my shoes were missing from where I had left them the night before. I did not know what to do.

How could I walk barefoot through snow and in the cold to the *Appel*? Who had done this to me? It had to be someone in the barrack, but who? I glanced around me, but nothing looked out of the ordinary, and I did not see the shoes anywhere. I began to panic. I started to scream. Someone had taken my shoes! In the confusion of the morning, everyone ignored me.

I ran desperately to the block senior. "Please, help me find my shoes," I cried.

"It's your problem," he answered gruffly. Then his eyes examined mine and he softened a little.

"Go to the rag pile, get yourself some rags for the *Appel*. Then we'll see," he said.

I ran to the rag pile quickly so that I would not be late to the *Appel* and took a few rags. I was the youngest person in the barrack and some of the older inmates felt sorry for me. Someone helped me wrap my feet in rags, and then we tied the rags together with some string. At least I had a temporary covering for my feet in preparation for the morning *Appel* and for the workday.

But I needed to devise a way to obtain shoes. Like our tin bowls and spoons, which we kept close to our bodies at all times, even at night, a prisoner in this camp could not function without shoes. We were forced to run outside all the time — from barracks to *Appel*, from *Appel* to work, and anywhere else we had to go. Punishments were severe if we were not quick enough. The SS would shoot a lingerer, or the *kapos* would beat him severely. It was winter and the ground was frozen. There was no way to survive without shoes as a barrier between your feet and the snow-covered ground.

That day at work, I was terribly upset. I decided I had no choice but to approach the manager of the shoemaking workshop and ask for his help. I told him what had happened to me and asked if it was possible for me to obtain a pair of wooden clogs. He promised me that he would speak with the SS man who was the inspector for our workshop. I sat nervously all day awaiting a decision.

When the inspector finally arrived that after-noon, I was called over to his table and the manager showed him my feet, which were still wrapped in wet rags. The manager showed the inspector an example of my work and said that my work was consistently perfect.

For three days, I wore rags on my feet. I kept two sets: one to wear, and the other as a replacement. When I arrived at the workshop in the morning, I would dry my wet rags near the stove and wear my replacement rags. I could not dry my rags at night, however, because the stronger people in the barrack controlled the stove and would not let me near.

Finally, three days later, the inspector approved my request for clogs at the manager's recommendation. To my surprise and relief, I received a new pair of wooden clogs that fit me perfectly. I felt my life had been saved. That relief and happiness carried me through the first couple of painful days while my feet adjusted to the strange new, flat clogs.

Shoes were extremely important, but at that time, nothing obsessed me more than food. I was hungry all the time. The 800 zloty I had brought into the camp were gone within two weeks or so of my arrival — traded on the black market for small amounts of bread. After the money was used up, I had no way to buy additional food.

I tried different techniques to relieve the hunger for a few moments at a time. I constantly debated with myself whether I was better off eating my entire portion of bread when I was given it, or whether it was better to save part of the piece for later, when the hunger would gnaw at me.

I also tried to fool my body by slicing my small portion of bread in half. That way I could enjoy the bread for a longer period of time and tease my body into believing it was being given two pieces. The piece of bread in my pocket never lasted long. I would constantly break off a small piece and it would disappear within seconds.

At one point, I felt that my starving body was in need of salt, so I traded, over a period of several days, a half portion of my bread ration for a small cloth bag filled with black cooking salt. I sliced my remaining portion of bread into three parts, and spread on each a small amount of the salt like it was butter. This made me thirsty, and I drank water to satisfy my thirst.

Eventually, however, my body reacted with rage to this salt. One morning, I felt something strangely wrong with my legs. I looked down at them and they were swollen like dough. They felt like they did not belong to me. They seemed to be weights separate from my body. I tried to put my feet into my clogs and they did not fit. I had to stuff them in like rags.

I became sad and cried bitterly. I had seen others who had become swollen like that, and they had died shortly afterwards. I lost hope for myself and felt that I, too, was facing the end. I tried to find a hiding place because I did not want anyone to see my misery.

I finally decided that I had to try to overcome this serious problem. I did not want to die. I was still young; maybe I could find a way to survive. I remembered my mother's optimism in the face of the worst possible events and I started to talk to myself.

I developed a technique in which I imagined that the war had ended, that I had returned home to Radom, and my family was gathered there. We shared with each other the stories of our survival. My mother would be baking *challah*, and frying cutlets, and the smell would be in the air, erasing the pain. Life would be sweet, like honey.

I tried to find a corner where I could be alone to escape the constant noise and confusion of the camp. I wanted to find a retreat where my mind could enter this dream world. This ritual helped me gather strength to convince myself that it was worth fighting to survive.

I found a wooden bench beyond my shoe workshop, within sight of the barbed-wire fence. I sat there when I had spare time. From this bench I could see outside the camp. I saw birds and trees. The birds sang. I felt jealous of them. Why were they free to fly all about, while I was imprisoned inside electric wires?

Each morning and evening, I recited the prayer that my Rabbi had taught me as a young boy in the *cheder*. The prayer was called *Kriyat Shema*, in which I expressed my faithfulness to God. I was hoping that God would hear my prayer and would help me to overcome my misery. The praying provided a mechanism to overcome my depression. I stopped eating the salt and the swelling slowly disappeared.

Others were not so lucky. Disease and starvation overcame them. Perhaps they were not as young and strong as I; perhaps they gave up hope. Maybe it was just bad luck. People were dying every day, and I saw their bodies carried out on wooden stretchers by inmates whose job was to bury the dead in the woods.

Accompanied by two Ukrainian armed guards, they would pick up the body, place it on the stretcher, and carry it outside the camp gates. With the help of a third inmate who carried the shovels, they would dig a grave and drop the body inside. This sight was so commonplace we stopped paying attention to it. But the first time that I saw a body being taken out, I wondered whether I would have a turn on the stretcher.

I was younger than almost everyone in the camp. I did not have any friends, did not trust anyone, yet longed for companionship. I wanted to share my experiences with someone. Others had friends, or occasionally a family member who had survived the deportations. I was jealous. Those who had friends or family were lucky because someone could help them when they were in trouble or felt sick. They made each other stronger.

In the women's section of Blizyn, I did have some friends. Esther Finkelshtein was there, as was Edzia Tepper, Pola Mandelbaum and Fela Vishnya, Mathis Vishnya's niece. These women had been close friends with Chaya. I used to play with Pola's youngest brother, Pinchas, who allowed me to ride his brand-new bicycle in return for telling him Bible stories. These friends were a few years older than I, but I felt they were attached to me. I could trust them.

I met them occasionally on the *Appelplatz* or in the public areas in the camp. One evening, I even went to their barrack to talk with them. We sat together on their bunk. I enjoyed this diversion. We talked about Chaya. We spoke of Radom and of our homes and friends. We expressed hope that we would all return there someday.

"Selections" of inmates for transportation occurred quite often here. A rumor would spread throughout the camp immediately prior to a selection. We did not know exactly when or how it would occur, but a rumor of a selection caused panic and a flurry of activity. Sometimes there were escape attempts just prior to a rumored selection. The inmates were usually caught and shot, in the *Appelplatz*, in front of the whole camp. This was done as a warning to the rest of us.

Others tried desperately to obtain additional food so that they did not look so emaciated. The worse a prisoner looked, the greater his chances to be selected for what we now knew was certain death. I had little chance of obtaining additional food, so I feared the selection process more than I feared being beaten by a *kapo*. On the morning of a selection, during the *Appel*, we would be notified that a transport would be leaving that day. We never were told the destination. Certain groups of inmates were ordered to remain standing after the roll call and were told that a selection would start afterwards.

The camp doctor, an SS officer, and a *kapo* would walk in front of each row of nervous inmates. The doctor would silently motion, with a finger, into which direction the inmate should run. Those who looked the most emaciated, or who limped, or who otherwise were sick, always were sent in the same direction. They were sent away, never to return. Later, they were replaced with a fresh group of prisoners.

Occasionally a request would come in from another camp for workers who possessed certain skills. Plumbers, carpenters, tailors, and shoemakers were sometimes in demand. These workers would go through the selection process, but because they were needed for the workshops, they were not as likely to disappear. One day, I heard that my women friends from the AFL had been sent to Auschwitz in such a transport. These were the only friends I had — the only connection to my past. I felt a great loss.

As spring 1944 arrived, I felt a little better. The warm air and the sun brought me comfort and hope. Along with the rest of the prisoners who worked in my workshop, my career changed. We stopped making shoes and began repairing leather or canvas bags for the German soldiers. We now were working in shifts because of increased demand from the front. I began to work the night shift.

During this shift, a *kapo* and an SS soldier came to our workshop and counted us while we worked. During the night shift, SS inspectors carrying whips and pistols came into our workshop to check our productivity. The man who sat next to me was from Bialystok. His name was Benjamin, and he had a beautiful singing voice. We enjoyed singing together Russian songs, which we were able to sing in harmony. The rest of the workers appreciated our singing because it helped to keep them awake through the night.

One night, I was exhausted and had just about finished my quota. We had been singing most of the night, but we had stopped. I fell asleep. Usually, when an SS inspector was about to enter the workshop, there was a signal from anyone who saw him. The manager would shout in German, *"Achtung!* Attention!" This evening I did not hear the signal or the manager's alert.

The inspector quietly entered the workshop,

walked up to the podium from where he could view the entire workshop, and saw me sleeping. He came straight over to me, stood behind me, and without warning flung a whip across my back and neck. I jolted awake, in shock, and began to pick up my needle, but he kept striking me with the whip. I covered my head with my hands so the whip would not hit my face. After about five or six blows with the whip, he then left the room without saying a word.

I knew that my punishment was not over. It would be continued later on the *Appelplatz* in front of the entire camp. The camp authorities loved to make examples out of people who were caught doing something like falling asleep on the job.

Nervous and angry with myself for falling asleep, I approached the manager at the end of the shift. "Did he take my name?" I said.

He replied with words that lifted my spirits. "No, you are lucky. Your name was not registered." This was unusual. I had never seen a worker escape punishment for such a "crime." *Beshert?* I began to wonder if my mother was not a prophet. Even though my back was in enormous pain, and I had large dark, ugly bruises all over my ears, neck and back, I thanked God that I had only received the six blows and that it was all over.

As much as I appreciated the coming of spring, the warm weather brought serious problems as well. Lice began to appear as spring turned to summer. A terrible plague, the lice attacked us in our bunks at night. Beginning in April, they appeared first in my hair and then all over my body. They were small bugs of a light beige color. When I sat in the sun during the day, I removed my jacket and peeled the lice off my clothes. I killed them by snapping them between my thumbnails.

They kept me awake all night, scratching until my skin bled. I was not able to get rid of them, no matter how I tried. Occasionally, we would be permitted to go to the disinfection room, a special barrack set up to rid us of the lice. First we stripped off our clothes, then we ran under cool showers and within a minute, would be ordered to another room to air-dry. We were given no towels. We stood while a man threw powdered DDT onto us, which we spread through our hair and all over our wet bodies. We retrieved our clothes, which by then had been disinfected through a heat process. The hot clothes felt comforting.

These efforts to rid ourselves of lice were in vain. The lice did not leave. They left their worst mark, however, not on our peeling, itchy skin, but by transferring typhus. Weakened already by horribly inadequate food, and unable to get medication or even to rest when we were sick, many contracted this disease and almost no one recovered. Some people who developed typhus were sent to the camp hospital. The hospital did not cure, however, and most people who were sent there did not return.

One day I began to feel hot. My head started to ache. I felt feverish and thirsty. I kept reaching for water. As terrible as I felt, I continued my work because I was afraid to report to the hospital. I felt so sleepy that I could not keep my eyes open. Next to me in my workshop sat a man named Mendel who was an expert at the work we did. Mendel noticed that I was feeling sick. He had gray hair and glasses that he used to wear on the tip of his nose.

As the afternoon progressed, I could not stop myself from dozing off. I became so weak that I could not even hold my head up. This wonderful man, Mendel, actually did the work that I was unable to finish. He woke me up gently whenever someone would come into the room. He forced me to drink liquids and kept refilling my bowl with water. He spoke soothingly to me and comforted me. This continued for three long days.

When I was not at work, I did not have anyone to help me. I forced myself to eat my bread and soup. The *Appel* was particularly difficult. I concentrated all my energy to walk to the *Appelplatz* and stand on my feet. I was pale, hot with fever, and shivered the whole time. I even felt that I might pass out. But I knew that this was a crisis I simply had to pass in order to survive.

After the third day, I decided that I needed help to reduce the fever and thought maybe I could get some aspirin from the camp hospital. I stood in the line at the hospital after work, and when it was my turn, I requested that the doctors admit me. They looked at me and said that there was no room. They gave me an aspirin and sent me away.

While I was standing there in line waiting to see the doctor, my mind wandered. I was home in Radom. My mother was there. She put me to bed, covered me with a heavy quilt, placed two pillows under my head, gave me a cup of honey-sweetened tea, and hugged me. She did not leave my side until I was asleep and she would be there when I woke up. I wanted her badly. I wanted this all to end and to go home to my family.

When I walked out of the hospital, I saw an SS man accompanied by two *kapos*, one of whom was from Radom. His name was Szlamek Minzberg. The head *kapo*, he was known as a cruel and terrifying man who constantly tried to impress the Germans with his brutality. Everybody in Blizyn hated Szlamek. If we saw him walking in the street, we took a different route to avoid him.

When I saw these two *kapos* that day, they were screaming at and kicking a man who had been standing in the line to see the doctor. The SS man was watching. The rest of the patients began to run away, fearful that they might be next. I also felt an urgency to get away, and I did, but I ran away as if in slow motion. I could not erase from my mind Szlamek's black, shiny boots kicking the sick man, who was lying there helpless on the ground.

That night I went to the *Appel* in a daze, feeling awful, but as soon as it was over, I went straight to bed, not even waiting for the evening bread distribution. Someone brought me my portion of bread and placed it under my blanket. The next morning I woke up completely wet. A miracle had occurred; my fever had broken and I felt better. I ate my bread from the night before and went to work, where Mendel immediately noticed that I felt better.

"Lyzerke, I can tell you feel a bit better," he observed.

"Yes, I feel better. I think it is a miracle," I told him thankfully. I also told him the story about my attempt to get admitted to the hospital and the doctors' refusal to admit me. He stood there looking relieved and a little perturbed at me for going to the hospital without telling him. I realized then how lucky I was to have him as a sort of parent, there when I needed him. He continued to help me, giving me an occasional dab of marmalade or a piece of bread. I don't know what happened to this wonderful man, but I really believe that he was an angel sent from heaven.

ॐ

Burek the *Soycher,* or "Trader," was a man who worked in my workshop, but he was known throughout the camp as a big businessman. He was about six feet tall and stocky, had red hair and a friendly, busy personality. He had energy that we all emulated. He was always smoking cigarettes, although we never knew where he obtained them.

Burek bribed the *kapos* and the guards so that he could trade with the Poles, the Ukrainian, soldiers, and with anyone else who might make him some money. He always had money and everyone knew it. He was never hungry. He was the main source in the camp for black market goods. Probably it was from Burek that my friend, Mendel, obtained the treats that he gave me when I was sick.

Burek was not careful in his constant dealings, and

he made deals indiscriminately. People warned Burek to be more discreet and to be careful with whom he was dealing. He used to say that the Nazis would "get him" sooner or later anyhow.

One day I was sitting at work shortly before noon. My chair was located near the sliding wooden door to the outside. The door was propped open. From where I sat, I could see everything that was happening outside. It was a sunny, pleasant day.

Burek obtained permission to go somewhere and I saw him leave our workshop. Within 15 minutes, I heard shooting outside. This shooting was not uncommon at night, but during the workday, we did not usually hear it so close to our workshops. The sound of the shots shocked us. We lifted our eyes and looked at each other. I had a feeling the shots were associated in some way with Burek.

Within 10 minutes, I saw a familiar-looking body being carried past the door. Four people carried him in the direction of the camp gate that led to the woods on a stretcher lifted high on their shoulders. Two armed Ukrainian guards and a *kapo*, carrying a whip, accompanied the stretcher. That was the last we saw of Burek the *Soycher*. It put an end to the huge operation Burek ran, which not only provided him with an income, but also brought badly needed black market items into the camp.

We lost friends every day, of course. People were murdered or died of disease or starvation all the time. But this death had an impact on most of us. Burek had always seemed so alive. He was young, strong, smart. Burek worked hard to make his life, and others' lives, better. He refused to give up — to be a victim. We talked about nothing else for days. We feared Burek's death signalled that worse times were ahead.

A few weeks later, we began to hear rumors of an imminent prisoner transfer. Rumors of an upcoming selection were always chilling. We knew that productive and healthy professionals would be transferred for work, and that unproductive, sick or weak inmates would be sent to Majdanek or Auschwitz.

I did not look well because I was not totally recovered from the typhus. I was weak and thin. Also, I was limping because of an infection on the bottom of my foot. Somehow, I had cut my foot and it did not heal properly because it was impossible to keep it clean.

I worried about being sent to the death camps along with the others. I still felt young and wanted badly to live. I was performing well at work, in part because the tasks involved sitting and working with my hands. I knew that I would not have been as productive if I had been assigned a job involving heavy labor, because I was still small.

Productivity didn't always necessarily matter to the Nazis. The selection, I knew, depended upon an inmate's physical condition in addition to his work skills. These factors determined whether an inmate was selected for life or for death.

One day in the last week of June, 1944, I went as usual to the *Appel* in the early morning. After we were counted, my block, along with several others, was ordered to remain on the *Appelplatz*. As soon as this order came, I knew that this day would be one of the most important in my life. I had to pass a test that depended not on what I knew or on how I acted, but on how I appeared to a total stranger who hated me.

I also knew that I must pass this test. We heard that the destination of the workers' transport was a camp called Plaszow. I knew nothing about this camp, except that they used professional workers like me. But I would have gone anywhere just to get out of Blizyn. I felt I could not survive much longer in this place.

All of a sudden, several *kapos* appeared along with Ukrainian soldiers and SS officers. Someone brought a wooden table with a small bench and placed it in front of our group. The *Blockschreiber* and the *Blockaltester* brought a file and began to call out names. When your name was called, you had to approach the bench, remove your shirt and announce your profession.

As I observed the selection procedure, I could tell that my chances for surviving the selection would be improved if I could demonstrate that I was strong, alert, and productive. Older people and those who walked weakly or slowly to the wooden selection table stood less of a chance. On the other hand, those who approached the table briskly, with confidence, and who answered questions in a loud voice, had a better chance.

Once the SS decided whether you lived or not, they notified you in a split second, with a flick of the thumb. As we watched the selection process, we could tell right away who would be selected to die because they looked similar: their faces lacked color, they were emaciated, they walked with apathy and lethargy.

When it was my turn, I walked as fast and as strongly as I could, hiding and trying to ignore the pain in my foot. With every step I took, my lips whispered a prayer to God that the thumb would point in the direction of the spared. I approached the table, stood stiffly at attention, and shouted my profession. Within a split second, it was over, and the SS officer pointed his thumb in the direction of the living. I shouted, *"Jawol,"* or "Yes, sir!" Excited, I ran over to the group and thanked God that my prayer had been answered.

When the selection was finally over, trucks arrived and the *kapos* shoved and pushed us into them. We were ordered to sit down on the floor of the truck, and Ukrainian soldiers, dressed in black uniforms, jumped in after us, pointing their rifles at our heads.

I felt a little hopeful as we drove away toward the cattle train that would transport us in a few hours to our new destination. It was June, 1944, the first time in almost a year that I was outside Blizyn's barbed wire. For a long time, I had longed to be free like the birds and squirrels that I saw flying and scurrying, without a care in the world, outside the camp's perimeter. Even though I could not see outside the truck in which I was riding, even the monotonous sound of the engine was refreshing after months in captivity. More than anything else, I felt hopeful because I was not headed for an extermination camp.

The Ukrainian soldiers confirmed that the name of our new camp was Plaszow, and that it was near the city of Kraków. We also heard that we would be working in similar workshops. Beyond this information, we knew absolutely nothing.

But I was unprepared for what was to happen. As we arrived, I realized that this camp was much larger than Blizyn. I saw all over the ground shattered remnants of Jewish tombstones. The camp had been erected on the site of a Jewish cemetery, which had been bulldozed to make space for the barracks; the beautiful old marble tombstones with their Yiddish inscriptions were cruelly and deliberately recycled as paving stones.

The camp was in a hilly area just outside the city. It was surrounded by a few pretty villas, one of the largest of which stood on a hill just above the camp. I learned that this was the home of the camp Commandant, Amon Goeth.

In the camp itself, all I could see were rows and rows of long, brown wooden barracks. These barracks looked different from those at Blizyn. Many of them were built on stilts to compensate for the uneven, hilly ground. The brown wood making up the barracks walls was interrupted every 10 or so feet by large, shuttered windows. These windows allowed light and air to penetrate the otherwise crowded, dirty, and smelly sleeping areas. The only color I could see in this camp was the red housing for the fire equipment outside each barrack. The bright red color contrasted sharply with the colorless nothingness that made up the rest of the place. The barracks were surrounded by double rows of electrified barbed wire. There were tall watchtowers manned by Ukrainian soldiers with machine guns. I could hear nearby the snarling and barking of angry dogs.

We were ordered out of the trucks and to line up in rows of five. Our welcoming committee approached us: the camp senior, several *kapos,* and an SS sergeant. They were different people from the guards at Blizyn, but the look on their faces was the same. They hated us.

After informing us of the usual restrictions and the range of punishments if we disobeyed the rules, a *kapo* ordered us to proceed to a special barracks for a search and a shower. As we ran to the showers, I was surprised to see a group of Hungarian women who, just a few days earlier, had been separated from their families and deported. They stared at us as we walked by, with eyes that still contained hope that they would find someone they knew. Most of us had been separated from our families for a long time by now, and we knew how they felt.

We proceeded into a large barrack, where we were ordered to undress and leave our belongings. After a brief, cold shower, I dressed again in the same old, dirty clothes that I had worn from Blizyn. I put my old hat on my head.

We quickly found out that the SS expected us to perform a sort of concentration camp dance with our hats. When we were ordered to the large *Appelplatz* for our first counting, we were already expected to perform this dance perfectly. The camp senior, first in rehearsal and then when Goeth arrived, ordered us to remove our hats in unison, shouting *"MUTZEN UP!,"* or "HATS OFF!"

When thousands of prisoners swung their arms and hats down to their sides all at once, it made an enormous whizzing sound like a momentary hurricane-force wind. If the sound was not just right, we had to perform the strange procedure over and over again until it was perfect. Then, we were ordered to place our hats back onto our heads with the shout, *"MUTZEN AUF!,"* or "HATS ON!"

In Plaszow, the roll call took a long time. We stood at attention for hours, waiting while thousands of inmates were counted, sometimes over and over again, until everyone was accounted for. If someone was missing, we stood there for hours longer, until the person was found and paraded in front of us, dead or alive.

Sometimes, an inmate became so exhausted that he would try to sit down on the ground to rest. If a *kapo* saw him, the *kapo* beat him terribly with his baton. I never sat down, no matter how I longed to, because I did not think it smart ever to draw attention to myself. I tried hard always to obey instructions.

Shortly after our first evening roll call in Plaszow, we were ordered to our new barracks, where we were assigned to a bunk. I was told to sleep at the top of a three-tiered bunk, next to Chaim and Lazer Tepperman, two young men from Radom. Then we received our bread ration. But now we no longer had our scale, and we needed to devise another system for fairly distributing the bread among us.

We chose a person to be the cutter, and that person, with our guidance as to how the loaf should be cut, proceeded to cut the loaf. Then we chose another person to distribute the pieces, but the distributer would hand out the bread blindly, with his back to the group, to ensure fairness.

I was terribly hungry after having eaten nothing all day, and quickly ate my bread portion. The bread did not satisfy me, so I tried to focus my attention on something else. Along with others, I tried to get information about where we would be working the next day.

Some inmates who already were staying in our block discovered that we would be working in the workshop responsible for repairing leather and canvas army sidebags or backpacks. This made me happy because the work was similar to what I did in Blizyn, and it would put us in contact with other inmates who might provide us with information about the camp. It could have been much worse because certain jobs at this camp involved hard physical labor, out-of-doors, where prisoners were forced to work regardless of the weather.

We knew that in the workshops we would have less contact with the camp authorities. Inmates at this camp bore a constant fear of contact with the SS men and the kapos. The camp Commandant, Amon Goeth, was a particularly brutal and cruel sadist. Goeth was young, not yet forty. He was tall and always dressed in a green uniform.

Contact with him or with his staff often brought immediate death. Goeth would personally shoot or have his dog attack and tear to pieces an inmate for no reason at all, sometimes only for appearing in the street at the same time as Goeth. If Goeth was spotted walking down a camp street or path, the way immediately cleared; the inmates knew that the mere presence of the man in the area meant a high risk that an inmate would be killed.

Many times I saw Goeth's favorite method of torture. He would approach an inmate in the street or during a roll call and motion with his right index finger for the inmate to approach. Goeth's thumb would hold secure his other fingers while the index finger summoned the inmate. Goeth would then shoot the inmate in the head. Goeth loved to sit on the veranda outside his villa and watch inmates through binoculars. If he did not like what he saw, he would shoot them himself or he would order them shot by his staff.

Goeth, his staff, and the *kapos* believed that our lives were totally valueless. Torturing or killing us was sport. Public hangings and executions were a regular occurrence. Punishment for an inmate's minor infraction often included the death or whipping of 10 or more other randomly selected inmates as well as the "violator," just to give a "lesson."

Killings that were not done on the spot were carried out either at the *Appel*, while all stood there forced to watch, or on a hill located on the outside boundary of the camp, called Cujowa Górka. This hill was the place where murders regularly took place of those inmates who became unproductive or those who were selected from the hospital as too sick to work. This hill was the place where entire families, caught hiding in the nearby Kraków ghetto, were murdered. We quickly learned to dread the sound of the words "Cujowa Górka."

In addition, the *kapos* and SS staff cooperated in putting together a corrupt and intricate black market operation where goods, including valuables, good-quality clothing and enormous quantities of food, were traded amongst themselves and the local Poles. This operation, led by the Jewish camp senior named Chilowitz and his deputy, Finkelstein, led to the establishment of a camp upper class made up of those who participated in this operation.

Some of these "protected" inmates even had their entire families with them in the camp. I was jealous of the children who were together with their parents. These people wore nice clothing and ate plenty of food, and contrasted dramatically with the rest of us. We were alone, wore rags, and were constantly hungry because the tiny camp rations were made even smaller by these corrupt individuals, who sold for their personal gain a large portion of the food that was earmarked for the rest of the camp inmates.

There was a group of fortunate inmates from this camp who had been selected to work and, in some cases, to live, outside. There were several factories in the area where private companies paid the Germans to utilize the inmates' labor. These inmates were treated much better on the outside, receiving adequate food and medical treatment, and avoiding the danger of passing in the deadly path of Goeth or one of his deputies. I heard that these inmates were chosen for work in one of these factories because of their connections or relationship with the head *kapos* of the camp. Others were chosen for their skills. I had neither connections nor skills.

One morning in July, 1944, after I had been in the camp for five weeks, I was alarmed to wake up feeling pains in my left leg. Afraid of the hospital because selections were frequently made there, at first I did not want to look at my leg for fear of what I would discover. When I finally looked at it, I saw a horrible-looking red, swollen area above my knee. I did not feel well and realized I was suffering from fever. I informed the block senior and asked whether I could see the camp doctor.

The Jewish doctor who saw my leg announced to the nurse news that was chilling for me. He said that this was a *phlegmona*, or an abscess, and that I would need an operation. This news hit me hard. I felt helpless and sorry that I had gone there in the first place.

It was too late for me to return to the barracks and to hide my illness from the block senior. I had seen people who had undergone this operation, and they did not always survive. The operation was carried out by German doctors who were interested in performing experiments on inmates. No drugs or anesthesia were given, it hurt, and it took a long time to recover from the trauma. During the recuperation time, the prisoner was unproductive in the eyes of the SS and was therefore a candidate for execution.

The nurse put me into a room in the sick-house, and told me to undress and to shower. After she gave me light gray hospital pajamas, she brought me to my room. This room was clean and painted white. I shared it with 12 or 15 other patients. We lay on wooden beds arranged singly, and we had straw mattresses with blankets. Polish and Jewish nurses took care of us. I was given some kind of drug twice a day and was ordered to drink it. To this day, I have no idea what this drug was. The Jewish nurse who took care of me liked me and kept telling the other nurse how cute I was.

I lay there for about five days and to my great luck, no selections were made from the hospital while I was there. Each day, the doctor would look at my leg and say that maybe I would not need the operation after all. The pains began to go away and the red swelling subsided. On the fifth day, the nurse told me that I would be released the next day.

My happiness at having survived the *phlegmona* and the hospital stay was diminished by what I saw there. I will never forget this sight. My bed was in a position where I had a view, on my left side, out a window through which I could see a courtyard. This courtyard overlooked the access road to the Cujowa Górka hill.

During the day, every day, this hill was the site of executions that happened in front of my eyes. I could see people: men, women carrying children, old people, young people, whole families being shot as if they were birds at a shooting range. I could see only the tops of their bodies as the people were led to the crest of the hill.

I heard loud orders to *"Feuer!,"* or "Fire!" and then I heard the "Ta-Ta-Ta-Ta" sound of automatic gunshots. The people would fall out of my sight into a ditch on the other side of the hill. Sometimes, I could hear a child crying just before the shooting, but usually the victims were silent. Many of these victims were not camp inmates, but Jewish families from Kraków caught hiding from the SS.

As the days of my hospital stay passed, I became more and more depressed by these scenes. I tried not to watch, but the sounds of the executions brought my eyes to the hill even against my will. It was torture for me to see and hear this day after day. Some of the victims were my age. Others reminded me of my own family. All of them were there one minute and gone the next. It was horrifying.

After I was discharged from the hospital, these scenes haunted me. I could not stop reviewing the killing scenes in my mind. I tried to concentrate on my work, but it was difficult to think about what I was doing. I kept hearing the order, *"Feuer!"* and then "Ta-Ta-Ta-Ta." I kept seeing the German faces enjoying the shooting; the bodies falling. I could hear the babies crying and then their silence.

During the summer of 1944 in Plaszow, we began to hear war news that brought us hope for the first time.

The Russians were advancing and the Germans' eastern frontier was beginning to crumble. As the Russians captured a number of cities in Poland, the Germans began to retreat. Although this news was encouraging, we wondered how these events would affect us Jews. Would the SS, in their desperation, kill us before we could reach our freedom? Would we be sent to the extermination camps?

Soon rumors began to spread of the liquidation of Plaszow. I thought this meant the end for me. I was sure that my destination would be Auschwitz or Majdanek. I hoped that somewhere there would be another labor camp that would need us.

After lunch on a hot August afternoon, we were called to the *Appelplatz*, and we were ordered to line up according to our work units. The SS and the *kapos* began to shout at us to hurry up into our places. As we gathered, we saw SS men arriving in open cars and shouting instructions to the *kapos*. Additional SS men and Ukrainian guards suddenly appeared in the yard with their guns.

Women from the women's camp gathered with us on the same *Appelplatz*. This was unusual because we were segregated from the women. As we lined up we saw a group of women led out from the *Appelplatz* to the right, and then to the left, where they disappeared from our sight. Within minutes, we began to hear machine-gun fire in the direction of where the women had walked. For five horrible minutes we heard the shooting, and then silence.

We then saw another group of women directed out of the yard. Again, after a few minutes we heard the

Clockwise from top:
Shvarlikovska Street in the
Radom Ghetto, 1993; Father
in a portrait taken for relatives
abroad, 1919; Father as a young
soldier in the Russian Army

Top: Zalman's Restaurant occupied the space behind the windows on the right; Above: Mayer Hershenfis at 17, dressed for a wedding. Radom, 1932.

Santa Maria, Italy, October, 1945, before leaving for Israel. Eli is second from the left in the back row.

*Right: Eli in the
Israeli Army, 1949.
Below: Eli, 1949.*

*Left: Eli (bottom, left) with
friends at the Chavat Halimud
Agricultural School in 1946
before the May Day Parade in
Jerusalem. Above: On the sea
voyage from Italy to Haifa. Eli
is on far right.*

Clockwise from left: Saying goodbye to Hershel, now called Tzvi, as he departs for America; Rivka and Eli at Chavat Halimud Agricultural School, 1946; Eli's family today: sitting, left to right: grandson Omri, Rivka, grandson Almog, Eli, granddaughter Neta. Standing from left to right: grandson Gil, daughter-in-law Hanna, son Ofer, daughter Nurit, son-in-law Yaacov, granddaughter Yifat; Hershel in America, 1948.

staccato sound of machine guns and then silence. Panic spread throughout the *Appelplatz*. People began to move out of the lines and to talk among themselves. Goeth, seeing the panic, started shooting into the crowd and people screamed.

Suddenly, orders came for all of us to lie down on the ground. We were warned that if we lifted our heads, we would be shot. Several people were shot. I tried to bury my head in the ground like an ostrich, and if I could have made myself disappear, I would have. I was terrified.

We lay there for some time, and the shooting finally stopped. We were ordered to stand up in our places and not to move out of the lines. Darkness began to fall, and we received an order to march out toward the railroad tracks. As we proceeded, we could see cattle trains waiting for us on the tracks ahead. At that point, even the familiar sight of these trains, which made me shudder at the memory of the trains that carried my mother and sister from the Maryvil station, comforted me because I would have done anything to leave the awful shooting scenes.

The SS and some Ukrainian guards lined up on both sides of the path to the trains. We were ordered to run quickly to the trains. Suddenly, I heard loud shouting and laughing as the SS and the Ukrainians began to have their fun. As we ran helplessly by these guards, they shoved into our bodies the butts of the rifles they were carrying. The blows were hard and they hurt. Many people fell down from the sheer force of these beatings and once they were down, the guards gleefully beat them some more until their blood ran down the path. I ran over bodies as I made my way to the train.

I darted to the train like a rabbit, trying to jump from side to side to avoid the blows of the rifle butts. It was like a horrible obstacle course. As I was about to jump into the closest train, an SS officer delivered to me the worst blow of the day. He shoved the rifle butt into my ribs and for a moment, I saw stars. Somehow, I made it into the train and crawled to the back on all fours. I was sure my ribs were broken and I could not even sit up. I managed to find a vacant space along the wall of the train. I could hardly breathe from the pain, but I was so relieved to be out of that hell, it didn't matter.

The doors were slammed shut. We sat in the train for a long time but finally it began slowly to move away from the ramp. The sound of the steam-engine was comforting because it meant we were leaving. But I had no idea where we were going.

Were we being sent immediately to the gas? After the day's experiences, I thought maybe it would be a relief to proceed straight to an extermination facility like Auschwitz. I was not sure I wanted to live even one more day if it meant I had to repeat those horrible events.

❧

The dirty, wooden railcar fell silent as we each considered what might happen to us. We were exhausted from the day's events, it was late afternoon, and we were hungry and desperately thirsty. Our train carried many people, and each car, like mine, was crowded. Two small windows near the ceiling provided the only light and fresh air. The cabin smelled from a terrible combination of urine, feces, powdered chlorine, and human misery.

About two hours later, as darkness fell, the train finally stopped. Rumors began to spread in our car that we had arrived at Auschwitz/Birkenau. I had heard that name many times before — its very sound evoked an image of mass death and suffering. But I also had heard that it was a place where there were workshops for skilled laborers. Except for the pains in my side, I was not unhealthy, and I did not look as terrible as some of the others. So I was determined not to worry whether or not I would be selected for death. I also had no friends or family with me, so I had no one else to worry about.

Our car sat outside the Birkenau gate for hours. Many other former Plaszow inmates were not so lucky. Their train cars were unhitched from ours, and sometime during the night they proceeded slowly through the infamous arches of the largest death factory in Poland.

Night arrived. It was hard to rest because I was anxious to know where we were going. The eerie calm we felt that night, stranded outside the barbed wire, contrasted horribly with the tumult and confusion inside for the new arrivals. As we sat there, many newcomers in similar trains passed our still one. The only sounds we were able to hear were loud orders in German or Polish to the trainmen outside the gate. The trains that proceeded inside dumped their doomed human cargo, turned around empty, again proceeded slowly past us, and on to somewhere else.

Finally the train slowly began to move. To my relief I felt that it was moving away from the camp. With the increasing speed of the train I was certain of it. My relief was soon mitigated by the increasing heat. I became more thirsty and delirious with hunger. The pain was shooting up my side so that I could not sleep. Finally we arrived at a station in Czechoslovakia, and the train stopped.

After a long while our doors opened and we began to cry for water. We could see civilians standing outside, mainly trainmen, and many SS guards with dogs. The guards allowed two inmates to empty the overflowing waste bucket, and distributed to each of us some water from a metal milk can and a piece of bread.

The doors then were slammed shut. We proceeded like this for days. About once a day the doors were opened, and those of us who were still alive were allowed some water and a portion of bread. Many did not survive. Older or weaker inmates could not bear the intense heat, the stench, the overcrowding, and the lack of food, air, and water. Their emaciated and dehydrated bodies were carried away at each stop.

The ride was bumpy. The train shook our bodies like popcorn kernels in a hot-air popper. The constant jolting became painful, especially for me. Even those of us who had been young and relatively healthy were dazed the entire time. But we tried to find out where we were going.

Eventually I heard that we were travelling in a southwesterly direction toward Austria. Sure enough, we arrived in Vienna. The doors opened and something unusual happened. As the water and bread were being distributed, a small group of nuns happened to walk by the train. They must have realized as soon as they saw us that we were camp inmates, because they immediately began to throw some apples into the cars. I never had a chance to receive one; I heard the Nazi officers yelling at the nuns that feeding us was forbidden.

Our final destination was Mauthausen, a small village in the Austrian mountains. We arrived at a small railroad station near the beautiful Danube River. The village was charming — it consisted of small, well-kept homes nestled securely in groves of trees. We could see many SS men standing on the platform and all around the station. They shouted at us to line up in rows of five.

My muscles ached from days of sitting in a cramped position. My whole body, in fact, felt like a piece of wood. No matter how I tried, I could not get my legs and arms to move the way I wanted. And I was exhausted and terribly thirsty.

But the air was fresh and clean, and the sky blue. This place was lovely. It was not long after we started to walk that I realized that the beauty of this place was illusory. The SS, accompanied by wild barking dogs on leashes, shouted at us to hurry. Those who fell or fainted were shot on the spot.

We marched along a narrow path up a steep hill.

As the walk became more difficult, the weaker fell behind. Many of the stronger inmates attempted to help the others up the hill. On the top of the hill I saw an enormous grey stone fortress or castle. Somewhat delirious from the train ride, I became excited. I had always wanted to visit a castle. I wished my sister were with me because she would have enjoyed visiting an ancient castle. We would have entered and found armored soldiers on horses, a colorful king and beautiful queen with their servants at their sides. From the distance I could not yet see the barbed wire that would remind me that this "castle" was not one that I was visiting as a schoolboy on a holiday.

As we got closer, I could see huge watchtowers manned by SS guards with machine guns. Other guards stood high above us on thick stone walkways, carrying submachine guns strapped over their shoulders. We were forced to run underneath these walkways and through a thick, heavy wooden gate. We ran as fast as we could, but those who entered the gate too slowly were pushed and shoved by kapos and struck with their batons. Those who fell to the ground were beaten until they lost consciousness.

When the commotion died down, I found myself in a large courtyard surrounded by high stone walls, barbed wire resting menacingly on the top. Guards patrolled the perimeter, walking back and forth or standing inside special buttresses built to allow a better view of the prisoners below. I felt trapped and frightened when I looked up at the guards standing so high above, looking powerful and dominating.

The right wall and the wall straight ahead contained many large, arched wooden doors that were open. The left wall also contained arches, but they opened onto a long corridor. After the huge gate was shut, *kapos* began to shout.

"Take off your clothes! Leave them on the ground! Put your jewelry and watches in the box!" The *kapos* pointed to some wooden containers nearby. "Hats and shoes off! On the ground!" They were afraid we were hiding something inside the shoes and hats.

In this chaos, I had to turn over Chava's ring. I had not removed it from my finger in so many years, and now they were taking it from me. The ring was worthless — just a piece of metal — but I became sad. I thought about Chava, my home, and my friends. This ring had been the first gift I had received from a friend, the only object left from my home town, and I treasured it. I had shined it every day. With tears in my eyes, I threw it into the wooden box.

We marched, completely naked, up a wide set of stone steps into the main camp, and then down another set of steps into a huge shower and disinfection room. After we washed ourselves, we were shaved of all our body hair.

Then we were ordered to sit in front of the barbers and they shaved our heads in the Mauthausen style. First our hair was cut short. Then a two-inch-wide strip was shorn, with an old, dirty clipper, down the middle of our heads. The barber was rough, and many of us received bloody nicks. I started to bleed, and my head felt sore. Camp inmates called this haircut the *"Lizenstrasse,"* or the "lice road." This ugly and impractical haircut was designed to make sure that we were easily identifiable to townspeople and to our guards in the event we attempted to escape.

From there we proceeded to a registration table, where we had to provide our name, place of birth, and religion. If there was ever a doubt about whether one of us was a Jew, his naked, circumcized body revealed the truth.

We each received a worn-out, thin, light-grey pinstriped pajama top and a pair of matching pajama pants. These pants were huge on me because I was so small and thin. I had to tie the pants and tuck the ends in so that they did not fall down. We were given no shoes, underwear or hats.

We were ordered to the roll-call square, where we were counted. Then we were marched down a wide dirt road, past rows of long brown wooden barracks, until the guards shoved us into the quarantine area, a small, crowded, noisy, section separated from the rest of the camp by stone walls topped with barbed wire.

It was late afternoon. We were exhausted and our stomachs were empty. Locked inside the walls, we each rushed to find a small space where we could sit and lean on something. We had not sat down at all since we left the train. Some of the new arrivals collapsed on the hard ground. I found a space at the side of a barrack where I could rest. I wanted to be left alone, I did not want to talk to anyone.

Sitting there, I began to shiver. I wished for a warm blanket and a hot meal. Instead, the *kapos* ordered us to stand for another roll call. We forced our tired bodies back to our feet and stood in rows while they counted. Then they ordered us to form a single-file line to receive our bread ration. My portion was tiny, dry, and I did not even taste it because I gobbled it down in a split second. We also received a little water, colored like coffee, to drink.

Soon orders came for us to sleep. We expected they would assign us to a barracks where we could sleep on a bunk. Instead, the *kapos* ordered us first to line up in rows and then to lie down on the hard ground in front of the barracks. Pushed and shoved by *kapos*, we were placed into position on our sides, squeezed tightly next to one another like sardines in a can, one man's feet at another's chest.

Even if allowed, it would have been impossible to turn or to move our bodies. We were so tightly woven together that the removal of any "thread" would have unravelled the whole. The *kapos* warned us not to move or raise our heads. They hit us with batons if we moved even a muscle. *Kapos* ran on top of us in order to reach anyone whom they felt the need to punish. I winced when I heard the cries of the men trampled or hit. It was painful enough to lie this way on the hard ground for so many hours — the beatings made it unbearable.

The morning greeted us with dampness, but it was made even worse because many inmates urinated in their places, wetting those who were near. There was no latrine barrack in the quarantine area. We were forced to use holes in the ground in the middle of a courtyard area. The holes were outside in the open; no building sheltered them or provided any privacy. We waited in lines to use the few holes, but many could not wait because they suffered from diarrhea or other diseases. These sick people relieved themselves right on the ground. The area was like a cesspool.

We stayed over a week in this horrible place, with nothing to do, not enough food to eat, and filth and disease all around. Many in quarantine died during the night, and were carried out on stretchers the next morning. If your neighbor died, you had to sleep next to the corpse all night because you could not move.

During the day we tried desperately to gather information. What were they going to do with us? We heard about the quarries at this camp where inmates were forced to work, carrying huge granite stones on their shoulders, up a steep set of 186 steps, for no purpose at all. Starved and tortured, these prisoners hardly had the strength to walk up these steps, yet they were forced to carry a heavy load. Many inmates, unable to take it, hurled themselves over the side of the quarry pit to a bloody and gruesome death.

This frightened me. I was small, and knew I could not make it in this camp. I had not been forced to do physical labor like this before — all the time I had worked in workshops with my hands, or in AFL storerooms. Some of the granite rocks weighed more than I did.

From the moment we arrived here I noticed a horrible stench, like nothing I had ever known. At first I could not sleep because the smell was so strong. What in the world could this be? Was there some strange factory in this camp?

To my horror, I discovered the source of the stench. Bodies were being burned, just near our quarantine area. This camp contained a crematorium. I had heard that the Nazis were burning bodies in death camps, but I had never been so close to a place where dark smoke carried with it all traces of human beings.

I wondered how anyone could put a person's body into an oven. I wondered what happened to the ashes of these people. My parents had taught me that when a person died, that person's life was marked with a tombstone. The tombstone even contained a few words that described that person's life. When you wanted to remember a person, you could go visit the grave at the cemetery. My father used to go to visit his relatives' graves regularly.

This was a Jewish custom. We were superstitious; we believed that the soul of a dead ancestor could help bring us good fortune. If no traces of a person remained, then we were disconnected. With no visible evidence of our dead relatives, we had no chance to seek protection from their souls.

The idea of cremation was so repugnant to me and to all of us that I could not understand why anyone could feel differently. I concluded that the Nazis did not consider us to be humans. How else could they burn us?

As if this were not terrible enough, I soon learned that this place contained a gas chamber where they suffocated inmates who were no longer productive. I heard that the gas chamber was small, and disguised to look like a shower so that an inmate would be fooled into thinking that he or she would receive a much-welcomed wash.

I was unable to get the horror of the gas chamber out of my mind. I tried to imagine what thoughts passed through the mind of a person trapped inside. I wondered if my parents, my brothers, and my sister had died that way. I heard that it took 20 minutes to die in a gas chamber. Twenty minutes seemed a long time to suffer. I forced myself to erase from my mind the thoughts of my mother and sister standing in a gas chamber — thoughts unbearable to imagine.

One day, after receiving our bread ration, I was sitting in the warm sun trying not to think about my body aching from sleeping the night on my side or about my calloused feet, which hurt from standing on the rough ground without shoes. I did not have any friends in this place. I felt isolated. I would have loved a companion. Sitting around all day, for over a week, had been monotonous and exacerbated my misery. Every minute that dragged by made me hungrier. The food rations were reduced because we were not working, and I was becoming weak and exhausted. My hunger made my body ache and my feet hurt even more.

I saw a boy my age walking slowly past. I was

surprised to see him because most of the men in the camp were older. The boy was skinny, a little shorter than I, and his body was draped in the same thin oversized pajamas that I was wearing. He had sandy-colored hair that had been shaved like mine, very short. The thing that really struck me, though, was his incredible sky-blue eyes. I have never seen anything like them. They penetrated right through me.

"Come sit next to me," I invited. "What is your name?"

"Shlomo. What is yours?"

"My name is Lazer." He sat down and we began to talk. It seemed as if I had known him for a long time. Shlomo was Hungarian and he had been separated from his entire family, as I had. I was even more surprised to hear that he also had been in Plaszow. It was in a selection there that he had lost his family. His parents, his sisters, and his brothers were all sent to Auschwitz in a single transport.

Comparing stories for hours, we learned that we had a lot in common, but that we also were different. Shlomo's father had been a successful baker, and his family had been wealthy. Shlomo liked *challah* as much as I did, and his father used to make them at his bakery. We imagined how wonderful it would be to share one of his father's sweet, braided *challah*s.

Shlomo's family was very religious, and Shlomo went to a religious school where he had to adhere to a strict curriculum of Jewish subjects. Shlomo was amazed and a little jealous of my stories about playing soccer all day with my buddies and my summers in the country and by the river with my sister. Shlomo was my first real friend since I had left the AFL. We did not separate for more than a few moments after we met.

Arrangements were made to transport my group away. I hoped more than anything that my new friend could stay with me. After the noon rations were distributed one day, my group was ordered to sit in rows outside one of the barracks in the quarantine area.

A block clerk began to call our names out loud. To my amazement my name was first. "Hershenfis, Lazer," he shouted.

"From now on, you shall forget this name," he ordered me. "It is no longer your name. Now you are a number. You are 84991. This you must not forget."

The block clerk then handed me a package, and I went back to my seat next to Shlomo. When I sat down I opened the package to find a complete set of clothing, including, to my surprise, a pair of leather shoes and even socks. I was thrilled because I had not worn leather shoes and socks for two years. I noticed later that this really had been a miracle because everyone else received not shoes, but wooden clogs. *"Beshert,"* I thought to myself.

When everyone else had received their packages, the *kapo* ordered us to get dressed. Shlomo and I were pleased to have these new clothes, which were much heavier than the thin pajamas we were wearing. We noticed that our shirts and pants had been labeled with our inmate number. This was the first time our clothing displayed a number.

The gray-and-white striped clothes were much too big for us, and we had to roll up the sleeves as well as the pants legs, but it did not matter. We were relieved that the camp authorities had provided clothes for us because it meant they considered us to be productive — we were being sent to a new job. And my new shoes felt comfortable — for the first time in weeks my feet did not hurt.

ፈ

The next day, Shlomo and I were thrilled to be ordered to march together out of this place. The late-summer Austrian day was magnificent. It was not too cold, and the sun was shining. Shlomo and I walked with the others out of the heavy wooden gates of Mauthausen and down the cobblestone road toward the train station. The SS soldiers guarded us closely with guns and bayonets.

"*Schnell laufen!*" the guards shouted. "Hurry up!"

We were ordered to march in groups of five, with interlocked arms so that we stayed together. This was their way of ensuring that no one fell behind. The pace was fast — the SS guards were impatient. That was fine with me. The sooner we were away from this place, the better.

We marched through the village for about half an hour. I was amazed. How could life be so normal in the neighborhood of a concentration camp? The village was picturesque. Small farms and homes were scattered about the green mountainsides. Flowers, trees, and other greenery looked lush. The beautiful dark-blue Danube raced proudly through the valley below the village.

I saw farm animals — cows and chickens. I also heard dogs barking. Village women, dressed in colorful clothing, and well-fed children stared at us as we marched along. I wondered what they were thinking. We must have presented a spectacle, because as soon as they saw us parade by in our tightly-woven rows of five, the children ran closer to us and even climbed onto fences to get a better look.

Many were exactly my age. I was jealous to see some of the boys playing soccer in the backyards of their homes. Their mothers worked nearby, preparing their meals and washing their clothes. These boys slept in clean beds and learned in school. Maybe they even went away for holidays with their families. I longed to be like them. I thought of the fruit orchards where my mother, Chaya, and I used to spend the summers together. I remembered the sour cream, onions, and radishes my mother prepared for me, the games I played with Chaya, and the mushrooms I was forbidden to pick.

When we arrived at the train station, we stood for a roll call, where the SS guards satisfied themselves that none of us had escaped. Then we were ordered to board waiting trains. These trains were not the freight trains I had become accustomed to, but were ordinary passenger trains. The SS soldiers pushed us into the trains and squeezed us into the wooden seats.

As each car filled up, the doors were locked. We departed soon after we boarded, each car accompanied by four SS guards. We pulled away from the village and were immediately in the midst of the most beautiful country I had ever seen. Passenger trains provide a view, a luxury denied to cattle-train passengers.

Mountains, fertile green fields, and trees stretched as far as the horizon. Brown wooden homes and barns were quaint, well-kept and orderly, and the people we passed looked healthy. The Danube followed our route much of the way. The pure tranquility suggested by these scenes made me wonder whether I had arrived on another planet. But it also made me feel somewhat hopeful — and even a little like a human again. With real clothes and a people-train, and with the beautiful scenery, maybe the nightmare was finally over, and I would wake up in the protective arms of my mother.

Two hours later, around noon, I was jolted back to reality as we arrived in another small Austrian mountain village called Melk. Melk is famous for its beautiful old Benedictine monastery — a light-colored, domineering structure that is considered one of the most beautiful Baroque buildings in the world. I could not help but marvel at the beauty and calm of this place, and it all seemed so normal-looking. The sight of the Danube, however, which winds its way aggressively through the town, and which seemed to follow us here, reminded me that we were not in a normal place.

At first we did not see any evidence of a

concentration camp. The train stopped at a loading ramp near the station. We were pushed out of the train and ordered immediately to again form rows of five. We then waited while the SS guards counted us one more time.

We marched on a wide, dusty, and uneven path. I knew already that I was lucky to have my leather shoes in this place. Those inmates who were forced to march with wooden clogs had a hard time. It was easy to lose my balance because the road was full of ruts, and it was so dusty I couldn't see the road very well. The guards were watching us closely, and if one of us tripped or fell out of pace with the others, the guard would immediately hit him with his rifle butt.

We began to wind our way upward, and the hill became steep at times. We marched past rows of small neat villas and shops that lined both sides of the street. The townspeople stared at us as we walked by. They did not look surprised, however, and I assumed they had become accustomed to seeing inmates from the Melk concentration camp.

Three or four very long kilometers later, we arrived at the camp, a former military facility situated at the top of the hill, just outside the village. This camp looked strange. It was surrounded by electrified barbed wire, and I could see the usual guard towers manned with SS soldiers standing behind machine guns. But aside from this, the place was not similar to the other camps I had seen.

Some of the buildings were two or three stories

high, like apartment houses. Many of the buildings were partially collapsed because the American bombers, concentrating their firepower in the general area, had attacked the concentration camp about a month earlier, apparently mistaking it for a military base. Camp inmates were at work under heavy guard, clearing the rubble.

The Melk inmates looked at us hopefully, searching for a familiar face. But the guards and *kapos* soon shouted at them to stop staring and continue with their work. We were eager to speak with the inmates to find out about the conditions in the camp, but it soon became clear we would have no opportunity to talk to anyone.

We were ordered to proceed immediately to the *Appelplatz*. As we lined up in our places, we caught our first glimpse of the chimney of the crematorium. I looked at Shlomo, and he looked at me. This place might be beautiful, but the nightmare was not yet over, and we knew it.

We were counted, and then we received a welcoming speech by an SS officer. "You have arrived in Melk," he shouted. "You have come here to work in the tunnels nearby. You will be divided into three shifts so that the work will be carried out 24 hours a day. You will not be permitted to leave your group. If you attempt to escape, you will be shot. The wires around the camp are electrified, so do not even approach them. A curfew will be enforced, and you are not permitted to walk outside the barracks after this time. If you do, you will immediately be shot."

We were divided into blocks; Shlomo and I were in Block 11. We walked up a hill with the others and trudged wearily into the first floor of a two-story, long and high, brown brick building. We were registered by the *Blockschreiber,* a tall, blonde, freckled political prisoner named Christian.

Then we met the *Blockaltester,* also a political prisoner, short and athletic-looking, named Willie. Willie had once been a professional boxer, and his demeanor scared me at first. His small black eyes darted around with a quickness that earned him a certain fame in the camp. These eyes were constantly panning the barrack scene in search of his next victim, usually a poor soul who might have committed some grave crime such as returning to the soup line for seconds, folding his blanket improperly or arriving late to the *Appel.*

When provoked, Willie would approach the offender like a lion approaches his prey, slowly, savoring each precious moment before the bloody attack. Hands on his hips, Willie would begin to question the victim about the offense. Willie loved to prolong the agony for his victim.

Willie rarely could bring himself to wait long for an answer. Instead, his right fist would shoot like an arrow into the face of the offender. If the victim did not fall immediately, Willie would strike a second blow, with the other fist, as in the boxing ring. Sometimes a kick would follow, and then another, until the offender either passed out or managed to run away.

This scene repeated itself almost every day, and at

first Shlomo and I were afraid. But soon we realized that something strange was going on at this place. The camp leaders rarely picked on the boys, only on the men. They seemed to treat the boys a little better. We discovered why.

This was the first time I was in an all-male camp. Here, as in the other camps, there was sexual abuse, but the targets were young boys instead of women. Many of the *kapos* and block seniors participated in this "leisure-time" activity, and their victims — always the youngest inmates — received special treatment in return, such as additional food rations and occasional chocolates. Unlike the others, however, Willie was not interested in the young boys. Christian was his lover, and they both left the others alone.

We also met the *Stubendienst,* or room servant. It was his job to oversee the distribution of food, and to serve Willie and Christian. The *Stubendienst* showed us where we were to sleep. The wooden bunks, three tiers high, only 28 inches wide and lined with thin straw mattresses, each contained a small, worn gray blanket. I was assigned to the top bunk, and Shlomo to the bunk just under mine. We discovered later that these sleeping conditions were luxurious compared with other blocks here in Melk. In many others, two men were required to sleep in the same-sized bunk.

Two inmates then brought a barrel of watery soup into the barrack and we were ordered to stand in line. The *Stubendienst* gave each of us a thin tin bowl and a spoon, and then he served, with a small ladle, our soup ration. The soup was a little thicker than the soup we had been given in previous camps, and it contained some barley and even a little fat. But the amount was insufficient. We were terribly hungry and thirsty after our transfer from Mauthausen, especially from the long marches up and down the hills. I felt dizzy and physically exhausted, and longed for more of this soup. But I did not dare risk returning to the food line.

After lunch we were ordered to stand in line again. Two barbers appeared with clippers. We were ordered to sit in front of the barbers and, just as in Mauthausen, they renewed our strange *Lizenstrasse* haircuts.

Around 3:30 or 4:00 the next morning, the *Stubendienst* and the block senior woke us up suddenly and loudly by turning on the lights and yelling, *"Aufstehen! Zum Appel!"* or "Get up! To the roll call!" We were expected to jump out of our bunks immediately. The *Stubendienst* and the block *kapo,* baton in hand, stormed through the barrack to make certain we obeyed the order. The *Stubendienst* shook the bed and the *kapo* beat with the baton anyone daring to try to catch a few more precious seconds of sleep. The bodies of those who died during the night were carried out on a stretcher or in a blanket by two inmates selected at random by the *kapo.*

Although dead-tired and weak from the journey and inadequate food, when I heard the *Stubendienst* yelling and sensed the brightness of the lights, I immediately and automatically jumped up. The Nazis had trained me well to respond quickly to any of their demands. I had become a robot — I felt nothing and obeyed every order.

We had to run quickly to the latrine. As usual, I tried to be the first to arrive so that I would not have to stand in line. Many men had terrible diarrhea here in Melk, as in the other camps, and they could not wait. These men ran to the front of the line, begging to be admitted before the others.

"Please!! Let me go!! I cannot wait anymore!!" a sick man would beg.

Occasionally such a man would be permitted to run right away into the latrine. Most of the time, those at the front of the line would refuse to let him in.

"I also have to go," one would respond gruffly. "You wait in line with the others." These starving men had long ago lost any manners, or even compassion, that they might once have had.

As a result the sick man often soiled himself right in front of the others. This was a big problem because there was no time for him to wash his uniform, and there were no extra clothes. If a man's one set of clothes became soiled, he had no choice but to wear them anyway. He would smell terrible and would feel even worse. In a desperate effort to avoid these consequences, some sick men even tried to stop the diarrhea by plugging themselves with a piece of cloth or paper.

After we returned from the latrine block, we were ordered to fold our blankets and place them neatly at the head of the bunk. Then we stood in line for "breakfast" — a quarter ladle of lukewarm chickory-flavored water. We then were hustled outside, and ordered to march in rows of five to the *Appelplatz*, which had been brightly illuminated with electric lights. By now it was about 4:00 or 4:30 in the morning.

The *Appelplatz* was located in the center courtyard of the camp, and we were ordered to line up according to block. We stood outside for over an hour, and then we were marched outside the camp gate. Prisoners who made up the camp orchestra were stationed inside the gate, and their violins played sweet music as we marched out.

Marching in rows of five, with our arms interlocked, we were heavily guarded by SS soldiers on both sides. Some of these guards were accompanied by ferocious-looking leashed German shepherds. We proceeded in this formation down the steep hill, through the town, and finally onto the train ramp where we were forced to stand in formation for a long time, until a freight train arrived to take us to work. When we arrived in the village of Loosdorf, we had to march another couple of kilometers to the tunnels.

Our work here involved digging huge underground tunnels in the Loosdorf mountains. These tunnels, designed to house armaments factories for the German war effort, were buried far beneath the mountainous earth in order to protect the operation from Allied bombardment. The tunnelling operation intensified around the time I was sent to Melk because of a shortage of labor in Germany toward the middle and end of 1944.

Our work detail, involving about 2,000 inmates,

was named *"Schachtbau."* A small, round tin tag, which was attached to our uniforms with a pin, identified us as workers in this particular group.

The Germans employed civilian mining experts to direct these tunnelling operations. The SS inspectors and the *kapos* walked around constantly, to make sure that we worked a steady eight hours without a break, and that sabotage was not attempted. If one of these inspectors or *kapos* were to catch someone standing still and not working, he would beat him unconscious with a baton or a rubber pipe that was tied to his wrist as if it were a permanent part of his body.

We worked in three shifts of eight hours each. On my first day of work I was on the day shift. Shlomo and I arrived around 7:00 a.m., and were assigned to work deep inside a section of the brightly-illuminated tunnel. Some inmates worked with pneumatic drills, loosening the soft quartz sand from the walls and ceiling of the tunnels. Others shoveled the sand onto long conveyor belts, which carried it out of the tunnel. Shlomo and I were assigned this job.

This was backbreaking work, and it was especially hard to keep up a momentum because we were hungry. The usual meager concentration camp food rations were supplemented in the evenings with some cheese or salami and a large piece of bread. Nevertheless, the work was much harder than the workshops I had been used to in the other camps — for the first time, I was being forced to do heavy physical labor. So even the supplemental rations were not enough to satisfy my hunger.

We were already tired by the time we arrived at the tunnels for work. We had been awakened many hours before to stand in the *Appel*. We worked out a system so that we could take turns resting. The Germans watched the conveyor belt closely; as long as a sufficient amount of sand appeared on the belt, the guards were satisfied that we were working. We took turns shovelling so that we maintained a steady flow of sand. Some of the inmates were supposed to signal if a guard approached. Then we would all pick up a shovel and work steadily while the guards stood there, watching us closely.

About a month later, as I was shovelling sand onto the conveyor, a tall and strong senior *kapo* who the Germans nicknamed *"der Cygoiner,"* or "the Gypsy," approached our section along with an SS inspector. I could not see them because they were behind me, but I had heard the signal, so I knew that some guards were approaching.

Sensing their approach, I began to work harder, shovelling the sand in a rhythmic, speedy, yet efficient motion. Out of the corner of my eye I could see the inspector and the *kapo* standing behind me. And they would not leave — they stood there for a full five minutes. They began to chat with each other in a low tone, and I could not hear what they were saying.

The *kapo* ordered me to approach. *"Komme heire,"* he said to me, motioning with his finger.

With the shovel in hand, I approached them, removed my hat and stood at attention.

The SS inspector looked at me sternly. "How long

have you been working here?" he asked.

"About a month," I replied, worried. Why was he singling me out?

"How old are you?" he continued.

"Sixteen."

"Tomorrow you will be a *Spitzentrager* (bit carrier)," he announced. Then he turned to the *kapo* and ordered him to remove me from my shovelling job.

"*Jawol,* Herr Inspector," I said to the inspector.

"Go back to your work," the *kapo* ordered.

This was truly a stroke of luck — *beshert.* The job of bit carrier was an independent one, usually handled by younger or smaller inmates, who were responsible for carrying replacement drill bits to the five drillers in each crew. No longer would I have to shovel the sand. I only had to provide the bits when necessary. Most of the time I would not be needed, and I could just walk around looking busy.

Shlomo was jealous. He tried not to show it, but I could tell. "One day I will also be a *Spitzentrager,*" he would say to me hopefully, as he would march, totally exhausted, alongside me up the hill from the train tracks.

Soon more drills and drillers were needed as the tunnels were expanded deeper and wider. More drill bit carriers also became necessary. One day Shlomo came to me at the end of our shift. All excited, he reported to me that he had indeed become a *Spitzentrager.* This was a relief to both of us — we were sure it was a signal that better days were to come.

੩ੑ

That year, 1944, the most holy day in the Jewish calendar — Yom Kippur, the Jewish Day of Atonement — fell on Saturday, October 9. Shlomo approached me a few days before the end of September.

"Lazer," he said, "My religious friends in the block have calculated the dates for the Jewish New Year and Yom Kippur. Rosh Hashana is coming next week, and Yom Kippur follows. Yom Kippur falls on the Sabbath this year. We must fast together."

I liked the idea. It would connect me to my family and my life in Radom.

"How will we do it?" I asked. "We need to find some food for the last meal before the fast. We cannot observe Yom Kippur without eating a meal before the fast."

"I have an idea," Shlomo said. "We will trade our cigarettes for bread and potatoes. Then we will make some potato sandwiches. We can eat them at work, just before the fast begins."

We did just that. On the day before the fast, we traded our cigarettes, hiding in our pockets the bread and potatoes we received in return. Preparing for Yom Kippur gave me pleasure because it evoked memories of better days...

Days when I had a family with whom to share the holiday preparations — days when I could watch my mother moving about the house, cooking, cleaning, pulling out our holiday clothes, the special white tablecloth, and polishing our heavy silver candlesticks. On the day before Yom Kippur, my mother baked, with apples from our orchard, a special pie that we called a *fluden*. The whole house smelled of this pie. It sat on top of the brown cupboard, and I could reach it only by standing on a chair.

We ate our meal before sunset. The whole family would then leave together for the synagogue. On the way we visited our neighbors to wish them a good year, and that they be sealed in the Book of Life. At the synagogue I sat inside with my father for the beginning of the service. Then I would leave to join my friends in the courtyard. We played outside until the service was finished and our parents collected us.

Shlomo and I were assigned to work the afternoon shift on the eve of Yom Kippur, arriving at work by 3:00 pm. Just before sunset, we hid ourselves in a corner outside the tunnels and ate our potato sandwiches and white cheese.

We then prayed to God that we would soon be freed and returned to our families. I wondered where my family was. Was my father praying with my brothers? Was my sister helping my mother clean up the dinner dishes somewhere? We felt it was within God's power to decide, on this day, who shall live, who shall not, and we prayed, for the first time in many years, that God would forgive us for our sins and judge us with favor. I wondered why the Nazis felt they were so powerful that they could step into the shoes of our God and assume the awesome power of judging which of us should be permitted to live.

Later that evening, I became very thirsty because we had added salt to our potatoes. I forced myself to refrain from drinking water or from taking the evening meal that was delivered to us upon our return to the camp after midnight. Instead we traded our portion for some bread that we could eat the next day, and we went straight to bed. The next day we could no longer hold out. We were dizzy and felt terrible. When others were given food, we decided to take ours as well, and we broke our fast.

But we felt good about what we had done — that our short fast demonstrated our faithfulness to God and our belief that God would help us. We were hopeful that this would improve our chances to survive.

This experience strengthened the bond between us. We had become a family — Shlomo had become my brother. For the first time since I lost my own family, I felt I could trust another human being. I loved him.

The weather turned bitter cold. Although the camp leaders promised to provide us with warm winter clothes, the days passed without any relief. Most of us had no hat, no new socks, and no gloves. We were wearing the same shirts and pants we had been issued months ago in Mauthausen, and by now they had become pathetically thin.

As the weather became colder, the roll calls became brutal and seemed to last forever. We were forced to stand outside, sometimes for hours, shivering in the bitterness. It was colder on the train ramp, where we stood up high, exposed to the violent winds that roared mercilessly through the mountains. The trains seemed to arrive later and later as the weather turned colder, prolonging the frigid agony. This was a terrible torture.

To alleviate the pain from the wind, we learned to use each other as shields. I made a real effort to stomp my feet and rub my hands together in an attempt to prevent frostbite. Relief was not available in the barracks, either. They were not heated except for a small stove that warmed only the *Blockaltester's* area.

The bitter weather increased the daily death rate. Every day people died from exhaustion in the barracks and at work. I saw people carried out on stretchers all the time. But where were the bodies taken? I did not know.

Soon, the camp authorities put into operation a crematorium to dispose of the bodies. The chimney was clearly visible from my block. The black smoke became a permanent sight — like the mountains or the trees. I could smell burning flesh all the time. It was worse at night, when my nose itched from the stench. After some time, I got used to the smell, and it became a regular part of the camp life.

As winter 1944 approached, it became snowy and wet, and our conditions further deteriorated. The march to and from the railroad became treacherous as the roads iced up. Our faces were exposed to the snow as we walked, and we could not shield them with our hands because we were forced to walk in columns with our arms interlocked. Our thin clothes would become soaking wet, and would not dry for days, prolonging the misery. Certain privileged prisoners were able to warm their clothes on the

Blockaltester's stove, but being a child, I did not have that opportunity.

Work accidents were frequent. The excavated tunnels were not supported well, and walls collapsed, trapping and crushing people every day under tons of quartz sand. We took turns carrying their bodies back to the train on stretchers, leaving them inside the crematorium yard for disposal. Occasionally, workers would survive such an accident; they would be taken to the hospital, also on a stretcher, at the end of the shift.

One day I was standing on a ladder in the tunnel, trying to hand a new bit to a driller who stood on another level. It was the end of the night shift, and we were preparing to transfer the operation to the next crew. I felt myself falling from the ladder. My left foot landed first, and I felt a sharp, excruciating pain in my leg. Then I felt sand land on top of me as an entire wall fell onto my body. I was buried alive in the tunnel, and lost consciousness.

Someone pulled me out, fearing that the whole section would collapse, and I was placed onto a stretcher. I woke up feeling horrible pains in my leg. Sand covered my clothes and my face. I could taste it in my mouth and feel it in my eyes. I began to cry bitterly, fearful that, as this was the second fracture of the same leg, it surely meant the end for me.

I dreaded the hospital, and I knew that was where I was headed. Inmates carried me on the stretcher, first to the train and finally up the hill to the camp. We arrived at the hospital, in a separate section of the camp surrounded by barbed wire. They left me on the ground outside the hospital, along with others sick or injured.

Two or three hours later the commandant of the hospital, a dreaded man nicknamed *"Musicant,"* or "Musician," arrived with an assistant to register those he felt were truly sick. I was taken to a small rectangular room in which sick prisoners were crowded two or three to a 28-inch bed, beds stacked two tiers high, near the back wall of the room. There was one table on the right side of the door that supported the meager medical supplies. A doctor's bed also was squeezed into a corner of this room.

The place smelled from a terrible combination of human waste, body odor, and disinfectant spray. The patients in this room were in horrible shape. It was cold, and not all of them had clothes on. Some of the naked prisoners were living skeletons. Most of them appeared to be sleeping. Many were moaning.

There was no room for me in a bed, and I could see that my place would be on the floor where the overflow slept, in between the bunk beds. The floor was filthy — trash lay everywhere. I was taken off the stretcher and placed onto a pathetically thin, dirty straw-filled canvas mattress. My leg continued to send sharp pains, like lightening, up through my whole body.

Later, a Hungarian Jewish doctor named Dr. Balog came to me, removed my shoes, and began to examine my foot. Every touch caused me to scream out in pain. He then took some bandages, dipped them in some liquid gypsum, and wrapped them around my foot to form a makeshift cast.

"I know this will hurt, but it will just take a minute and then you will be all set," he comforted me.

The cast took time to dry, and my foot felt better. I felt hungry, so I reached into my pants pocket for the piece of bread I usually carried. It was still there. I ate it hungrily and fell asleep, exhausted.

The next day I woke up for the roll call, which took place in our room. Some of the skeletons had died during the night. The bodies were thrown onto stretchers, any gold teeth and their clothes were removed, and the stretchers were carried away. The remaining patients were given the morning coffee, but there was only half the usual portion — for those of us who were not productive.

Some days later I was moved to a bunk, which I was to share with two other veteran patients. One of them was an older man named Janush who was on the verge of death. As he was too sick to eat, we would forcefeed Janush some of his soup. He refused his bread completely, and the other man in our bunk greedily ate the whole portion.

The day after I moved to this bunk, I woke up with a strange feeling. Janush's body was totally still, and it felt cold against mine. I looked over at him in pure horror. His eyes were wide open, and they seemed to be staring at the ceiling. His mouth was grotesquely wide, as if he were struggling to take a breath of air. He smelled terribly, and body fluids were running out onto my bed.

Janush was dead. I looked around for Dr. Balog.

"Doctor, he died," I said, hoping the doctor would take the body away immediately and have the bed cleaned. I felt squeamish and horrified lying next to a stinking, skeletal body. But Dr. Balog glanced at the corpse for only a second and then walked away, expressionless, to continue his business. Dead bodies were as commonplace around here as were the bunk beds.

Not until many hours later was the body taken away — I had to lie next to it all morning. I tried to look the other way, to think of the body not as a person but as bones. I would have gotten out of bed if I could have walked.

The next day I was approached by a Hungarian patient, a little older than I, who was assigned to help Dr. Balog. This boy was named Hershel. In Yiddish he said to me, "The doctor would like your leather shoes. He will trade his clogs for them, and you will receive better treatment, including an increased food ration."

Realizing that I had no choice but to give up my valuable shoes, and hoping that the doctor would carry out his part of the bargain and provide me with extra food, I immediately agreed. Dizzy with hunger, and uncomfortable in the cramped, dirty conditions of the hospital, I hoped maybe this deal would prevent the doctor from assigning a third patient to our bed.

My shoes were wrapped inside my clothes, and I had been using the bundle as a pillow. I reached under my head for the shoes and handed them over. "You have made a wise decision," Hershel said.

From then on, I occasionally did receive a supplemental portion of bread. Dr. Balog moved me into Hershel's bed, whose mattress was thicker, and the blanket warmer. Hershel and I received a clean gown more often. Hershel arranged for me to be given a thicker portion of soup every day.

My pains slowly disappeared, but I could not yet walk. To get to the bathroom, which was just outside our room in the corridor, I had to hop on my right leg. I lay down all day, and really rested. It was luxurious compared to working in the tunnels.

I began to like the situation better and better, and hoped I could stay there for as long as possible. I saw patients discharged by the Nazi doctor every day. He used to come into our room with a list, and he would sometimes throw out patients whether they were better or not. I hoped I would not be discharged.

One day I mentioned to Hershel that I had once sung in the synagogue choir. He became excited right away. "Why don't you sing here? It will make the time pass a little, and it will remind us a little of our homes."

I was afraid. Singing was unusual in the hospital. Maybe it would bother the other patients, and worse, maybe a *kapo* would hear it and decide to punish me. My survival strategy was always to keep a low profile. Singing might call attention to me that could be dangerous.

I especially feared the Commandant of this hospital, the *Musicant*. He was not a doctor, but he ran the hospital, and we all were frightened of him. He used to kill patients by injecting air, benzene, or phenol into their veins. I did not want this madman to notice me at all.

Hershel convinced me that I would not be harmed. "Sing softly and nothing will happen to you. Maybe the patients will like it," he suggested.

I began to sing. I sang portions of prayers that I used to sing in the synagogue. I loved singing. It reminded me of my home, where we used to sing all the time. I sang louder as I realized that the others, especially the Hungarian doctor, actually liked my singing.

One day the Polish inmate responsible for food distribution heard me singing. He asked me if I knew any Polish folk songs. Of course I did, and I sang for him. He particularly enjoyed one funny song about patients and doctors: "Doctor, I am sick. Heaven knows what is wrong with me, appendix or something else. Just a few days ago everything was fine. Am I going to die?" "Tell me how much money you have," the doctor says, "so I'll know how to answer you."

I would sing for this Polish inmate every day, as he would serve the meal to the others. My singing pleased him so much that he gave me a thicker soup portion, taken from the bottom of the barrel.

With these improved food rations, I was able to save some of my bread. I tried to think of a way to smuggle some to Shlomo, who was still working in the tunnels. The *Stubendienst* from my block would come every couple of days to the hospital for record-keeping purposes. He carried messages between Shlomo and me in exchange for cigarettes, which I received occasionally. One day I gave him some cigarettes in exchange for his agreement to carry some bread and cigarettes to Shlomo. This strategy worked; Shlomo got a message to me that he had received the items. I sent bread and cigarettes again a few days later, and again got a message that the items were received.

This was a good situation. I was no longer hungry, and I could get some of the food to Shlomo. We both were excited about these improved conditions. Though I missed his companionship, I knew this was better for both of us.

One day Shlomo smuggled himself into the hospital compound and stood outside of the window next to my bed. He took an enormous risk to do this, and I was surprised and thrilled to see him. He was wearing a coat and a hat, which also surprised me because he had had neither when I last saw him. He waved at me happily. I motioned to him with my fingers a question: Had he received the cigarettes? He nodded that he had. We waved at each other and then he left.

A few days later, news came that there had been an explosion in the tunnels, during the night shift, in the *Schachtbau*. As the survivors arrived at the hospital, they reported bit by bit the alarming details. Many had been killed — either by the explosion or by the collapsing walls. But I could not determine the fate of my group, and I was sick with worry for Shlomo. Since I had been separated from my family, he had been the only person I trusted — he had become my family and my only friend. Was he alive? Or was my friend's body buried under the quartz sand somewhere deep inside the tunnels?

☙

The next day I discovered the gruesome truth. The explosion had originated in a tunnel where my section was busy working. Everyone in my team was either killed or wounded, even the Yugoslavian mining expert, a civilian.

My worst fear had been realized — Shlomo's body had been recovered and was taken, along with the others, to the crematorium. My best friend in the crematorium. I must go rescue him! He could not have died! I did not believe it. I cried for hours. My own small accident several weeks before, although it had been painful beyond words, had most certainly saved my life. If I had not broken my leg and been sent to the hospital, I would have been in the vicinity of the explosion. *Beshert?*

Stunned, I felt weak and empty. Not only had I lost Shlomo, but I realized how close I had come to finally meeting with death. Every night for a week I cried myself to sleep. I knew I was alone again, with no one to talk to or to share support.

My leg improved and the cast was removed. I was released from the hospital and returned to my block. Block 11 felt different without Shlomo and the rest of my group. I missed Shlomo, and cried tears of longing and bitterness. I knew no one could replace him.

When I felt so depressed that I almost gave up, I was again lucky. Before I returned from the hospital, the *Stubendienst* for my block had been sent back to work in the tunnels, and a new *Stubendienst* was needed. I was chosen, and was assigned my new duties.

My job involved taking care of the barrack for the block senior. Willie became my boss. I cleaned his room, washed his laundry, and served his meals, sometimes even preparing sandwiches for him from whatever was available from the kitchen. I woke up the inmates in the morning, and served the food to them.

The job provided me with many benefits. I no longer was required to travel to and toil in the tunnels. The winter of 1944 was brutal. Inmates returned from the tunnels exhausted, starving, and freezing. Many of them could not stand on their feet. It took all their energy to drag themselves to the barrack, and they fell onto their beds. It horrified me to see this suffering, and I appreciated my special conditions even more.

As the distributor of the food, I could serve myself thicker soup and extra portions of bread, cheese or salami. Sometimes I could find a boiled potato. I began to gain weight and to feel stronger. Color returned to my cheeks.

As a privileged inmate I also received warmer clothes. I was given a thicker jacket and a special hat. I was able to secure a pair of leather shoes from an inmate in exchange for a little extra bread. I was moved to a bed in the front of the barrack, and I was able to get myself an extra mattress as well as a second blanket. I had power, and it felt good. Other inmates in the barrack were eager to please me in the hope I would remember them at mealtime. If only I had Shlomo to share these benefits — then I could be happier. I tried to help other inmates as often as I could. I would give thicker soup portions to the weaker ones.

Winter passed. People died every day from starvation, brutal working conditions, and inadequate clothing. Winter clothes arrived late and were not plentiful. Many inmates had no coat, hat or gloves. It was nearly impossible to survive such conditions. The black smoke poured out of the crematorium chimney day and night.

At the same time, we were receiving encouraging information from the civilian tunnel workers and other outside sources. The German army was retreating to the west, and the United States army was approaching Germany and Austria. We also heard that some of the concentration camps in Poland had been liberated by the advancing Russian army.

Every night we heard the sound of airplanes in the sky. We knew they were the Americans, and we gained strength from the hope that they would finally and completely destroy the German army and arrive to liberate us. For the first time in years, optimism filled our souls, increasing even more as the snow began to melt in early April, 1945. The days began to lengthen, and the sun poured warmth upon our frozen gray bodies.

I thought about what I would do when finally freed. I would walk outside the electrified fence, find a loaf of bread, and eat the whole loaf. Next, I would return home to Radom. Someone from my family would be waiting there for me. I would resume my schooling. I would excel in geography again. I would make my parents proud.

I would enjoy my remaining childhood years. My friends and I would play soccer every day in the square. We would spy into the windows of Zalman's Restaurant. By now I was taller and I would have a better view. In the summer we would return to the orchards. Chaya and I would play *strulkies* by the stream. Maybe my sister would decide she was too old for *strulkies,* and she would insist we play something different.

The SS staff in Melk began to get nervous as the Americans approached and the German army retreated. They started disappearing slowly from the camp, apparently being reassigned to the German front lines. They were replaced by new guards taken from a unit of the German air force.

On April 14, 1945, the entire camp inmate population of between 8,000 and 10,000 men stood in formation at the roll call. The morning work shift had been kept in the camp. I could sense that something terrible was going to happen today. The SS Commander of the camp, Julius Ludolph, appeared in front of us and began to deliver a speech.

"Today we are going to begin evacuating you to another camp in Austria named Ebensee. This camp will be closed. You will continue to work in tunnels in the other camp. You will shortly board a boat to Linz, and then you will walk the rest of the way. Do not try to escape. If you do, you will immediately be shot."

We were ordered to remain in our places. Two SS doctors, accompanied by a group of *kapos*, walked through the *Appelplatz*, selecting the weaker inmates for transfer back to Mauthausen. I looked healthy thanks to my months inside as *Stubendienst,* so I was selected to accompany the first evacuation by boat.

I was ordered to leave in a column of inmates as if we were going to work. But instead of proceeding to the train, we marched a little further to a pier on the Danube, where there stood waiting large wooden tugboats. We were again counted and then shoved onto the boats, where we were ordered to sit on the wooden floor. So many of us had to be squeezed together into the boat, we were forced to sit with our knees pulled tightly up to our chests. I was able to support my back by leaning against the back of another inmate. This was how we were able to help each other in a small way.

As we slowly moved down the Danube, guards surrounded us, standing rigidly and holding rifles. *Kapos* milled around. If someone tried to stand up or stretch his legs, he was shoved back to the floor or beaten until he was bloody. I heard many gunshots, and was told that people were shot trying to escape and their bodies thrown overboard. The trip dragged on slowly and painfully. I was uncomfortable crouching. I felt like the bones in my back and in my legs were broken. I became hungry and thirsty, not having had a food distribution in many hours.

We were given a portion of watery soup later that evening, and I realized we would be spending the night on this boat. Darkness fell, and I dozed off. It was uncomfortable and I could not sleep well in a sitting position.

The next morning we passed a sign that indicated we were passing the town of Mauthausen, a place with which we were all too familiar. I thought that wherever we were going could not possibly be as terrible. I was glad that the tugboat did not stop there.

Finally, we arrived in Linz, Austria. Rushing us off the boat and pushing with their rifle butts anyone who was too slow or who stumbled, the guards shouted, *"Shnell, shnell!"* Ordered to stand in columns, we were counted and each was given a small loaf of bread, which we were told would have to last us two days. Then we began to march.

I forced myself to ration my bread so that I could make it last. I became terribly thirsty, and felt like my mouth was on fire. But there was no water for us. I saw some dirty snow on the side of the road. When the guards were not looking, I quickly reached down to the roadside and grabbed some of the snow in my hand. This way I was able to quench my thirst a little as I marched.

After marching like that a whole day, we arrived at a huge barn in Wels, Austria. Straw lay everywhere. It appeared to be a barn that ordinarily housed some farmer's sheep or goats. But there were no animals in sight, and certainly no people. It seemed that this temporary barrack had been well-planned — there was even a small area with holes in the ground to serve as a temporary latrine.

On our arrival we were given a small amount of soup. I was so hungry that I could not resist eating, within a minute, the entire meager amount. I ate a small piece of my bread, and put the rest in my pocket. At Melk, I had been accustomed to receiving almost as much food as I wanted, so these starvation rations were enormously unsettling. It had been several months since I had felt hungry. Now, I had no idea when or whether we would be given our next meal. This frightened me.

We were ordered to lie down on the straw. It felt good to stretch out my body, and I immediately fell asleep. I was awakened by the alarming sounds of gunfire. The guns must have been nearby, judging from the noise. I was too afraid even to lift my head, so I lay awake for a while until the shooting stopped.

The evening was chilly, even for April, and we had no blankets. I shivered for a long time, and tried to move closer to the next inmate to share some warmth. Finally, I must have fallen asleep again.

About 5:00 a.m., we were awakened by the *kapos*. "*Aufshtehen!* Get up!" they screamed at us. Anyone not springing immediately to his feet was beaten. I jumped up even before I realized how badly I felt — I was shivering from the cold, and my clothes were damp from sleeping on the ground, so I could not warm myself. I felt groggy from the restless sleep.

We were ordered to form the usual roll-call columns of five and were counted. We also were told that the shots we had heard during the night should serve as a warning to all of us — the shots had killed several inmates who had been caught trying to escape.

We were given a small ladle of lukewarm black water, ordered to form columns of five and rushed onto a narrow asphalt road. Guards and *kapos* marched along both sides of the column, screaming at and beating or shooting anyone who stumbled or fell behind.

At first the marching warmed me up and I was able to dismiss the hunger pains. After the first hour the pains became severe, and I felt weaker. I was not sure how I could make it further. My left leg, which had not been healed for very long, began to ache. As each hour passed the aching worsened and my leg started to swell. I began to limp. It was necessary to hide my limping from the guards so that I would not receive a punishing blow. It became harder to keep up with the others.

I felt frightened and lonely. A Hungarian boy my age, who I knew from Block 11, noticed my limp and encouraged me to continue. "You have to go on. Hold out for a while longer, and we will arrive. If you fall behind they will finish you off."

Finish me off. I thought about what it meant for them to finish me off, and I imagined being shot by the side of the road. I saw many bodies lying by the side of the road, and they looked dirty, bloody, and powerless. I began to cry. The Hungarian boy couldn't stand to see me crying and walked away, but as he did, he started to sob also.

I had to distract my mind from focusing on my leg pains and the hunger or I would not make it. I started to think about our final destination, Ebensee. Surely we would have bunk beds to sleep on, with mattresses. I would be able to rest. Our conditions would be good because they needed us for work. If they had not needed us, they would have finished us off already — we would be black smoke in the Mauthausen sky.

As we crossed the highway on our march, we saw truckloads of German soldiers retreating westward toward Salzburg. I convinced myself that this was a good sign, that the war must end soon, and that I only needed to hold out a little longer. Then I would be free to go home.

We passed beautiful towns and villages nestled in valleys below the still white mountains. The display of scenery distracted me a little. Some of the local people stood by to stare as we walked by. Only the elderly women seemed to pity us. Once or twice one of them attempted to throw us some bread, but they were quickly warned by our guards that such conduct was forbidden.

As evening started to fall, we were ordered to enter a large grassy area that was part of some kind of industrial complex. We were told that we would sleep there. By now my leg was swollen to almost five times its normal size. My left shoe was so tight I could not even remove it.

I was dead-tired. I had not eaten more than a ladle of watery potato-peel soup all day, and yet I lost interest in food. I do not know whether the others received a food ration that evening — I did not wait for it. After the guards counted us, I collapsed on the ground.

I lay there feeling paralyzed. I could not move,

could not feel my leg, and could not control my body. I wanted badly to go to the bathroom because they had not let us go all day, but I could not get up, so it happened right there as I lay on the ground fully clothed. I could not help it. My pants were completely wet, which made me colder that evening, but I was only semiconscious, so I really did not notice until the next morning that I was freezing.

As I continued marching that morning, the wet canvas-like pants rubbed like sandpaper against my thighs, which became red and sore. My left leg was still terribly swollen. Walking was torture.

Many people had already died from this ordeal, and more died by the minute. The bodies were thrown onto trucks that moved with us. Our pace had slowed drastically. We were starving, thirsty, exhausted, and sick. We were given no water, and very little, if any, food. Some inmates ate grass or leaves that they grabbed from the roadside. These poor desperate people became sick with diarrhea and stomach pains, which usually meant the end.

Rumors began to filter down to those of us who were still alive and marching that we would arrive at our final destination by the afternoon. I was encouraged by this news, so I trudged on.

A German sergeant named Gustav, who I knew because he had been in charge of Block 11 at Melk, approached me. I had known this sergeant well because he often used to bring me his boots to shine and his shirts, handkerchief and socks to clean. In the camp he had been a little different from the other Germans. He had brought me some biscuits occasionally in gratitude for doing his laundry.

I was walking on the far left side of the column, and for some reason a gap appeared between my row and the next one. Gustav quickly brushed close to me on my left. I could feel that he was handing something to me. It was hard, and I realized it was a big chunk of German bread. I grabbed it quickly and put it into my left jacket pocket. He pulled away and walked ahead.

I broke off bits of the bread so no one would notice and shoved them into my mouth. I felt better, and continued limping along.

In the late afternoon we approached the town of Gmunden, at the edge of a beautiful blue lake called the Traunsee. Townspeople on bicycles stopped to stare as we passed. We walked along the lake for over an hour, and then entered a forest. At the top of a hill we entered a gate supported by block pillars. We had arrived at Ebensee.

❧

This camp was much larger than Melk. We were told later that the population of the camp was increasing with the evacuation of others in the area, and that the addition of the almost 6,000 Melk evacuees swelled Ebensee's ranks to almost 18,000 by the end of April. Conditions of overcrowding and inadequate supplies were obvious. We caught a frightening glimpse of some of the inmates as we arrived. They looked emaciated, like skeletons, dirty and underdressed. Some had no shoes, wearing rags on their mud-caked, calloused feet.

The camp was located at the foot of a mountain, and tall trees hovered over the long rows of barracks. I was happy to arrive, despite my first glimpse of the horrible condition of the inmates, because I felt that anything would be better than continuing to march on my swollen and painful foot. I thought we were sure to receive a meal.

We were ordered to proceed to the *Appelplatz*. There we were not allowed to sit, but had to stand at attention until the entire procession had entered the camp gates. Like others, I was so tired and hungry I could hardly stand. Many collapsed on the ground, but were forced back to their feet by punishing blows of *kapos* with clubs. It took more than an hour for everyone to enter and form columns for the counting.

We were counted and registered, and the Jews were ordered to form a separate group. My group was taken to the disinfection barrack, where we were ordered to remove our clothes. I was upset to lose the warmer, softer clothes I had received as a *Stubendienst* in Melk, especially the jacket and the underwear.

We were pushed into the cold shower by *kapos*, who moved us along by hitting us with rubber pipes. But before we had a chance to wash our bodies, we were pushed out. We were given a worn-out set of striped canvas-like clothes, which we were forced to place on our wet bodies. Then we were ordered to proceed to the Jewish barracks.

The barracks were wooden, as were the bunks. The place was dusty because the sawdust-filled mattresses were worn and leaky. It also smelled terrible. Many inmates had uncontrollable diarrhea, which ended up all over the bunk beds at night. I was assigned to share a single bed in the middle of the three-tier bunk with another inmate from Hungary, who had arrived with me on the march. We dropped into our bunk and fell asleep right away. I could have slept for two weeks, I was so exhausted.

A few hours later I woke to the screaming of the *kapos*. We were ordered to jump up and proceed immediately to the roll call. After we were again counted we received our first "meal" in Ebensee. Dinner consisted of a tiny chunk of dry black bread and a small amount of watery soup made out of rotten potato peels. I could not eat the bread because it was so dry, so I broke it into pieces and put it into the soup. I devoured this meager meal in three seconds, and craved more food. I felt hungrier after I ate than before.

My leg hurt, and I fell back to sleep in pain. Early the next morning we were awakened, counted in the barrack, and given a small amount of chickory-flavored water. We went immediately to the nearby tunnels for our work assignments.

The mountains here did not consist of quartz sand, as in Melk, but of a kind of hard rock. The tunnels were referred to in the camp jargon as the "quarry." The work was completely different. Whole sections of the tunnels were exploded with dynamite, and we were required to work in groups of three, to collect into small wagons the sharp and rough pieces of rock with no tools but our bare hands. My hands bled from handling the rocks. Sometimes they were so heavy they had to be lifted by two or more people.

After filling our wagon, we had to empty it outside. The full wagon was heavy, and it took all three of us, pushing with our remaining energy, to move it down the track. To conserve energy, we tried to move as slowly as possible without provoking a *kapo*.

German guards and *kapos* always stood around us yelling and beating with rubber hoses or clubs anyone who did not work fast enough. The conditions in the tunnel were miserable. Water dripped from the ceilings, and collected on the tunnel floor, forming small pools. It was cold. Our feet usually stood in several inches of water. I tried to step on rocks to keep out of the water. Sometimes the rocks I loaded were wet and would slip right out of my fingers, narrowly missing my cold toes. We were allowed only one break a day, for lunch. We were given a ladle of watery potato peel or turnip soup. This meal was insufficient after the hard labor I was required to perform. I lost weight quickly, and became skinny and weak. My leg still hurt me all the time, and it swelled up after I had been at work for a short time.

The only respite was the five or so hours of rest we sometimes were permitted at night. But if we were assigned to work the night shift, sleep was impossible. We would arrive back at the camp at seven in the morning, but we were not allowed in the barracks because they were being cleaned. After lunch we were sometimes permitted to sleep for a few hours, but any sleep we managed to achieve was interrupted by the afternoon *Appel* and the distribution of evening rations. The result was tremendous sleep deprivation, which only the strongest could survive under the harsh working conditions and with the severe malnutrition.

The Germans were paranoid about inmates escaping into the forests. We were counted four times a day, sometimes more. The food rations were minuscule, and the work back-breaking. People were starving as I had never seen. Desperate for food, inmates ate leaves and other greenery found around the camp or along the path to work. Rumors abounded that pieces of coal were good to eat because they contained fats. Friends of mine decided to eat the coal, and they became very sick.

One inmate told me that a Russian inmate had given him some meat to eat one day. Shocked and thrilled to receive the meat, he ate it right away. Later the Russian told him the meat had been that of a human being. Inmates were eating people's bodies in this camp.

Inmates were sick with all kinds of diseases, producing uncontrollable stomach cramps and diarrhea. Once you became ill, it was impossible to get better. Conditions in the hospital were terrible, so sick people preferred to remain in the barracks. People were dying by the hundreds, every single day. We became accustomed to seeing bodies lying everywhere. The crematorium worked

24 hours a day and still could not accommodate all the bodies. Piles of corpses began to accumulate near the crematorium building, eyes and mouths open as if they were screaming upward to the heavens.

It was difficult to distinguish the dead from the living, as they began to look eerily alike. One time a friend of mine woke up in horror to find that he was lying in the middle of a heap of naked skeletons on their way to the crematorium. He opened his eyes, thinking for a moment that maybe he had died. Pinching himself to make sure he was still alive, my friend realized that he had been mistakenly thrown on a heap of bodies after he had fainted. Somehow he managed to crawl out of the horrible pile and sneak back to his barrack without being detected by a guard.

Toward the end of April, the tension increased tremendously for the guards and the *kapos*, and they became even more cruel to us. Beatings increased, on the slightest pretext or for no reason at all. We heard airplanes flying high above us, and in the evenings we could hear the music of heavy artillery, which we knew meant the Allies were defeating the Germans. When darkness fell I could see the horizon become flame-red with the exploding artillery fire. This made me happy.

After about two weeks in this camp, I was transferred to another job, which involved pouring concrete. This job was worse than the last because the wet concrete was heavier than the rocks. I was forced to walk in the concrete eight hours a day. It hardened on my legs, and I couldn't get it off. My shoes felt like casts.

Too tired to wash ourselves after working in the tunnels, we were filthy. One rainy, windy, and chilly night after midnight we were awakened to sounds of *kapos* screaming and hitting the bunk beds with their clubs. We were ordered to run immediately several hundred meters to the disinfection barrack. We were not allowed to put on our shoes or our clothes.

I forced my body out of the bunk and ran barefoot through the thick rocky mud in the direction of the disinfection barrack. All of a sudden I felt my legs collapsing and I landed in the mud. I could see a *kapo* yelling at me to get up, and swinging a club in the air in my direction. But before he could hit me I scrambled back up and ran.

We were ordered to put our clothes into the disinfection oven, and then pushed into the shower, where I was able to soap my body a little before I was pushed out. I retrieved my clothes and shoes, put them on quickly and ran back through the mud and cold rain, to the barrack.

One beautiful sunny day I thought I heard the sound of airplanes flying overhead, and I noticed many inmates looking up toward the sky and pointing. I saw a beautiful sight — thousands of white leaflets dancing downwards from the sky. Most of them did not fall into the camp, but we knew what the contents must be — the leaflets contained messages from the Allied forces to the Germans that the end was finally near and that surrender was the only alternative.

Rumors began to spread. The morning of May 4,

1945, I heard that the camp Commandant, Anton Ganz, had received orders from Berlin to destroy all evidence of the camp. We were to be marched to the tunnels, and once we were inside, the tunnels were to be dynamited. A camp underground movement had discussed plans on how to respond in the event such an order was implemented.

That morning, I was terrified by the rumor that the tunnels would be exploded. I was willing to risk a beating and to forego my lunchtime food ration, which we received only in the quarry, in order to avoid going into the tunnels that day. Along with hundreds of others, I pretended to be sick and fainting. People lay all over the ground.

The SS guards, as well as the *kapos*, having become increasingly fearful of their own fate in the face of what now appeared to be their certain defeat, began to lose control for the first time. The guards and *kapos* ignored us and made themselves scarce. We were able to wander freely around the camp. I walked around or sat in the sun most of the day, eager for information. I was excited but nervous about what the guards might do to us as the end drew near.

The next morning no one was called to work. Instead inmates lay on their bunks until about 7:00, when the familiar clanging sound summoned us to the *Appelplatz*. As we were called to attention, I saw the camp Commandant stand on a table or a chair so that we all could see as well as hear him. Ganz was surrounded by SS guards wearing helmets and carrying guns. He began to deliver a speech, which was translated for us.

He told us that the Americans were nearby and were bombing the area, and that they were getting closer to Ebensee. There would surely be a tank battle between the Americans and the Germans, he warned us. Our only chance to survive the battle was to be sheltered in the tunnels. He said our guards had prepared a shelter for us in a tunnel where we would be completely safe. We should prepare immediately to march in columns to the assigned tunnel.

The camp underground had prepared us for this possibility, and we knew what to do. All of a sudden a voice yelled at Ganz: "No! We are not going!" Then another voice repeated the protest. In many different languages the "No!s" and other expressions of refusal became louder and louder, swelling finally into a chorus. I joined the chorus, thrilled to participate in what felt like an uprising. For the first time, we were actually refusing to obey an SS order. I felt more powerful than I had in years. At the same time I became afraid, and looked in the direction of the guard towers, certain they would open fire on us. The others fell silent, waiting for the SS response.

But to my great surprise they did not fire. Our response seemed to strip Ganz and the other SS officers of their power. They looked meek and confused. Ganz had a short conversation with some of his staff, turned to us, said a few words about the shelter plan being designed for our own protection. Then the entire group of SS soldiers turned around and walked away.

I was happy. I felt that the winds of freedom were blowing in my direction. We stood around the *Appelplatz* for a long time, talking. Some shared cigarettes. We also shared the feeling of having won a victory over our captors.

A few hours later the SS walked out of the camp forever. Some fled in cars; others rode motorcycles. As they left, the guard towers were filled by the *Volkssturm,* the local national guard. But the inmate underground committee took control inside the camp. Warning that it was too dangerous to leave, the leaders of this committee urged us to wait for further orders.

But some of the inmates could no longer control themselves. They began a block-to-block search for the *kapos* and block seniors who, collaborating with the SS, had carried out orders to kill or beat the inmates. I saw inmates running around the camp, wild and out of control, carrying sticks, rocks or huge tree branches.

When they would find a former collaborator, inmates by the hundreds would attack, tearing his body apart limb by limb, and crushing it with the heels of their wooden clogs. I could see brains lying on the ground. I saw the *kapo* from Melk, who had been known as the *Cygoyner,* lying headless in the dirt. Other former *kapos* or camp leaders were drowned in a pool, the bodies left floating for all to observe. One of the camp seniors was killed by hanging. The perpetrators of these gruesome acts were so out of control they lashed out at symbolic targets as well — at one point even pulling down an empty guard tower.

We stayed in our barracks that evening, afraid the SS would return and open fire. All night I could hear machine guns and artillery fire close by. When dawn broke I had a feeling I would be freed that day, but I was too hungry to think about what I would do upon my liberation.

All morning we walked around together, waiting for our liberators. I hoped it would be the Americans — I had heard a lot about Americans and had loved western movies as a small child. I was certain they would bring food. We had not eaten anything in many hours, and I was still determined to eat a loaf of bread all by myself.

Early that afternoon, as I was standing with the other inmates in the *Appelplatz*, waiting impatiently for something to happen, we heard the faint sound of heavy vehicles moving through the forest toward the camp. As the sounds grew louder and louder, many ran to the front gate to see who was approaching. I wanted so badly to run over to the gate to be the first to see our liberators, but I was too weak to run or even to fight the crowds. So I waited in the *Appelplatz* as hoards of laughing and screaming inmates streamed to the gate.

A beige-colored tank, which had burst through the front gate of the camp only moments before, came to a stop in front of me. Then another tank appeared.

"The Americans are here," people shouted in many languages. "We are free!"

PART SIX

Liberation

We cried and hugged each other. I could not believe this was actually happening, so I pinched my arm and then my cheek to make sure it was real and that I was alive on this great day. Hundreds of crazed, filthy, skeleton-like creatures with shaved heads jumped onto the tanks until the helmeted American soldiers gently forced them back down, and then themselves jumped to the ground.

Inmates tried to touch the soldiers to make sure they were real. In the confusion and excitement, bursts of song erupted from groups of inmates. National anthems in many languages could be heard. Some of the inmates held flags from their countries. As the soldiers watched this scene in horror and amazement, some of them began to cry. They gave out cigarettes, biscuits, and cans of whatever food they had. The inmates who were lucky enough to be handed these items ran away to eat or smoke. Most of us received nothing.

I decided to see if I could find something to eat. I walked to the kitchen and the storage room, but could not find even a scrap. Other inmates had already been there and taken whatever they could find.

While I was searching the storeroom, I found a boy my age named Hershel. I was happy to find he was also from Radom; his sister had worked with me at the AFL. Together we decided to leave the camp to find something to eat. As we walked outside the gate, I saw that others had the same idea — a river of emaciated, filthy, yet exuberant inmates was rushing to leave, all streaming madly toward the village of Ebensee.

Outside the camp for the first time, I felt as though I were in a different world. I saw villagers — mostly women, children, and the elderly—standing guard over their homes. They were afraid of us. Some of the mothers pushed their children inside; we looked threatening in our desperation.

Some of the villagers waved at us and smiled. We just ignored this self-serving, phony friendliness. Where had these people been when we suffered in Camp Ebensee? They had been our neighbors, yet in their silence they had collaborated with our captors.

I could think only of food. Some inmates approached the villagers in the hope they would give us some food. And some were rewarded with a scrap here and there. These lucky ones ate fast, stuffing their mouths with the food like a beast in a jungle would devour its prey.

I was jealous of the ones who found food, because I could find nothing. Even the side streets were overflowing with blue and gray stripes, and I was not anywhere near the front of the crowd. There was no way there would be anything left for me. Finally Hershel and I came to Steinkugel, a deserted workers' camp that had housed the civilian workforce for the tunnels. This place was a five-star hotel compared to our camp, and we were excited to have stumbled upon it. Running into a barrack, Hershel and I found a room with four beds. The beds actually had real mattresses and pillows, luxuries I had long ago forgotten about. There were showers and a kitchenette. We tore open the cupboards but could find no food. Then on the kitchenette table we saw a few small stonelike chunks of dry black bread. We wet the bread with water so that we could chew it, and ate it quickly.

Darkness had fallen. We realized with some alarm that it was too late to find anything more to eat. Needing a place to sleep, and determined not to set foot in the Ebensee camp ever again, we decided to sleep in two of the four beds. We were joined by two more Jewish survivors who, welcomed by our Yiddish, decided to stay in the two remaining beds. Still terribly hungry, we felt even hungrier when we saw others cooking, on open bonfires, food that they had been lucky enough to find earlier that day.

Next morning I heard voices over megaphones requesting that we register to receive food. A committee of former inmates, under the direction of the Americans and the Red Cross, was already organizing what had become a displaced persons camp. I registered, and considered going outside with Hershel to find food, but I felt too weak to move. I only weighed about 55 pounds.

By noon a truck arrived with the first shipment of food. I was served a ladle of thick soup that had meat in it. I was given a large slice of bread. There was not enough for us to receive seconds, but I felt stronger already.

After I had eaten a little, I wanted nothing more than to erase all evidence of my captivity. I decided to wash myself, but the lines for the washbasins were very long. So Hershel and I found a little river nearby. We had no soap, but we took off our shirts and began to splash the cold, clear water over our upper bodies. We began to enjoy ourselves. We splashed each other and laughed like little children. We pushed each other into the shallow water. We swam a little, and then sunned ourselves on the riverbank. The sun warmed us and we felt good.

I dozed off a little in the sun. When I awoke it was summer, and I was in Poland again by the river near our orchard. Chaya was there with me, and we were racing our little homemade paper boats. We were laughing and giggling. Suddenly, a gigantic wave raced down the river toward us. We had no time to run. My sweet, beautiful sister disappeared from my sight, the wave swallowing her like a giant monster. I managed to swim ashore and started to call her name. "Chaya, Chaya!" I shouted, but I couldn't see her. All I could see, as I caught my breath on the riverside, was a glimpse of our boats, crippled and overturned, yet floating far away from me. Then they, too, fell out of sight.

Worried, Hershel shook me awake. He said I was

shouting a name in my sleep — it sounded like "Chaya" or "Chaim" — and that I was crying.

"I had a bad dream," I told him. "It was nothing." I did not want to talk about it.

We decided to return to the camp to find some dry clothes. After a short search, I found a white jacket that appeared to have belonged to a German army cook. I tore off the German insignia and slipped on the jacket. I found some pants that were much too big for me, but I was very happy finally to discard my inmate uniform with the number 84991. I did not want to be an inmate anymore.

Later that evening we received another meal of porridge, tea, and bread with margarine. We were more than satisfied to receive these meals of rather bland food. We knew they were designed to ease us back to health. But we longed for certain treats, such as an egg, cheese or chocolate. We wanted foods we would be free to cook ourselves and eat when we wanted. We had been forced to adhere to someone else's schedule for too long. Now that we were free, we wanted to keep our own.

The next day Hershel and I decided to search for our own food. We discovered that we were permitted to travel on the trains for free and that food could be found in the nearby towns and villages. Carrying canvas sacks we had found in the camp, we went to the station, hopped a train, and got off a few stops later. Other former inmates, easily identifiable by their strange "lice road" haircuts, joined us on the train.

After a long walk, we reached a red-roofed farmhouse. Smoke was billowing out from the chimney, suggesting to us that someone was cooking inside. As we approached the house, a dog started to bark. Then an old man wearing a green hat with a feather on the side appeared. He had a pipe in his mouth.

"Good morning," he greeted us kindly.

"We are former inmates from Ebensee," I said to him in German. "We are hungry. Could you give us some food?"

"Sorry..." he started to say to us. But, seeing the disappointed looks on our faces, he added, "Yesterday we gave away most of what we had. I will see what I will find."

The farmer went inside without inviting us in. I think he was afraid we would rob him. Then he came back outside with half a loaf of homemade bread.

"Maybe you have some potatoes or onions?" I asked in a pleading voice. "What about cheese? Surely you have some."

I wanted to store some food so that I could eat it without waiting until the next meal. I wanted something to cook for myself. And I wanted certain things — foods I had not seen in years. If I could only eat certain things, I could convince myself that I was truly free.

"Nothing," he answered me in a polite voice. "There is no food left here."

Disappointed, we walked further to a small town called Bad Ischl. The town looked inviting and did turn out to be hospitable. I saw many former inmates also looking for food and just walking around. I also saw American soldiers walking or riding vehicles. Many of these soldiers were on duty, helping the town's police maintain order.

Someone gave us a bag of dried potatoes, and we found some yellow cheese, half a loaf of stale black bread, and a few onions. At one house a woman brought outside some old clothes for us and placed them on the ground. Eager to get rid of the German clothes I was wearing, especially the jacket, I selected a green long-sleeved shirt and a heavy gray winter jacket. They were both too big for me, but I was very happy to receive them. Any clothes were better for me than German ones. I did not want any association with Germany or Germans.

Satisfied, we proceeded to the train station and returned to the camp. We heard that a delegation of Jewish soldiers from Palestine, members of a unit called the "Jewish Brigade," had been in the camp that day looking for child survivors. They posted notices on bulletin boards, with detailed instructions for any children who might be in the camp to contact the Jewish Brigade through an immigration center that had been set up in Salzburg. The Brigade would provide assistance to children who wanted to emigrate to Palestine.

Hershel and I could not decide what to do. Information was coming in rapidly about various options. Our names had been placed on lists along with those of thousands of other survivors all over Europe, and these lists were published in Camp Ebensee. We decided reluctantly to make a trip there. I hated the place and never wanted to see it again, but I hoped desperately to find someone from my family on a list. I wondered whether there was a chance that my brother Abush or my father could have survived. Both had been among the last to leave the ghetto, and both had been considered productive workers. Maybe they had ended up in a labor camp as I had, and maybe...just maybe they were somehow alive.

Alphabetical lists of names were posted in the center of the camp, where an administration building had been set up to deal with the thousands of survivors. I ran up to the bulletin boards, squeezed myself through the crowd of people searching for names, and quickly scanned the lists until I found "H." Anxiously, I searched the lists of survivors with the initial "H," but could find no Hershenfis listed anywhere. Disappointed, I turned and walked away. I was jealous of people who found names of relatives.

On my way back out of the camp I noticed that the place looked very different. It had been cleaned up; no longer could I see bodies lying all over the place, or smoke coming from the crematorium chimney.

Powdered chlorine had been spread on the ground to disinfect it. Red Cross ambulances were eva-cuating the sickest people to the town's hospital. Hospital tents were set up for those who were well enough to be treated on-site. Nuns and other civilians from the town of Ebensee were helping the Red Cross in treating the sick. Many people became extremely ill from overeating in the days following the liberation; a lot of them died.

American soldiers were walking around everywhere. Some were supervising clean-up operations being carried out by German prisoners of war. It pleased me to see the captured Germans cleaning up the filth they had created. I was told that it was these German prisoners of war who had removed from the camp and buried in mass graves the thousands of bodies that were lying around. Some of the former inmates jeered at them.

The former inmates were still skinny but they had been provided with showers, so they didn't look as dirty. Many were still wearing their concentration camp uniforms, but I could see that the uniforms had been cleaned. Apparently new clothes had not yet arrived. I was happy to be wearing civilian clothes and to have somewhere to go. I did not want to remain in this camp.

Hershel and I returned to Steinkugel. We found many people organizing groups of former inmates to return to their homes. One group was returning to Poland, and we considered going back to Radom to see if we could find our families. I was not sure what to do, and became confused. I had to make a decision for myself for the first time in many years.

Hershel and I talked about it for many hours, and also consulted with others. We decided, finally, not to attempt to return to Poland. We were afraid of being on our own, and we decided the chances were slim that we would find anyone. We decided our best option was to join the group of children being taken care of by the Jewish

Brigade. But we had missed the registration. Somehow we had to get to Salzburg.

A few days later we were excited to discover that a small group of Jewish survivors had found an old van and were preparing to drive it to Salzburg. We pleaded with them to permit us to join them. They agreed, and the next day we departed after lunch, Hershel and I facing backwards with our feet dangling outside.

As the van drove off, we could see our barracks and even the barbed wire, which had encircled the civilian worker camp, become progressively smaller. Hershel and I watched in silence the fading reminder of our torn-apart lives, and hoped never to see the place again.

In a few hours we arrived in a village called Strobl. After years in awful captivity, we longed to enjoy nature, to be surrounded by beauty. This picturesque place seemed just what we wanted. Near a small, lovely lake named Wolfgang See (also called Abersee) were some deserted barracks, and we decided to stay for the night.

Hershel and I walked down to the lake, and found a comfortable place to rest at the water's edge. In the distance we could see and hear the sounds of children playing with their parents on the shores of the lake. The sun was shining brightly, and I wondered where the sun had been for so many years. It did not seem real, and it did not seem fair that these children enjoyed sunshine and had their parents while I did not.

The next day we found in the village a Red Cross food dispensary for displaced persons. Our identity cards, which we had been given at the workers' camp to show we were former concentration camp inmates, ensured our entry, and we ate a cooked meal. Then we proceeded to Salzburg.

In Salzburg there was a huge refugee center for Jewish survivors, run by the Jewish Agency. I was relieved to see trucks and soldiers from the Jewish Brigade. We went to the registration office, filled out some forms and answered many questions. An officer wanted to know in which camps we had been, where our hometown was, and whether we had any family anywhere. He asked where we wanted to go. Both Hershel and I did not hesitate. We did not want to go back to Poland. There was nothing for us there. We both wanted to go to the Land of Israel.

We received our living assignments and were told to watch the posted notices, which would provide further instructions. We received identity cards. We were refugees now, no longer camp inmates.

The place was overcrowded with refugees, and there were not enough beds to go around. Hershel and I had to share one. I noticed with amazement that every day groups of 25 or 30 children were evacuated by British army trucks. Most of these children were orphans. I found out that the groups were being taken by soldiers to someplace in Italy, and that from there they were going to youth villages in Palestine. And most amazing to me was that the soldiers conducting this clandestine operation were Jewish volunteers serving in the British army in Europe.

I became impatient waiting for my turn. I was anxious to see the place that I had imagined as a child contained sand dunes, camels, and date palms. I wanted to go to Jerusalem, to see the holy city. I spent several sleepless nights worried that I would be left behind. On our third day in the refugee center, Hershel and I went to a sergeant of the Jewish Brigade who was in charge of the children's transports.

"Please, Sergeant," I said to him. "We are only two travelling together, and we have been waiting for three days now to be assigned a space in a truck. We are willing to sit on the floor, if there are no seats available."

"Maybe tomorrow there will be space for you," the sergeant promised us. "Come back and I'll see if I can find you some space on the next convoy."

The next day our names did not appear on the list. Hershel and I were near tears when we saw that the sergeant had not kept his promise. We appeared at the parking lot and found that five or more trucks were already loaded with skinny children with happy faces. Hershel and I approached the sergeant and reminded him of his promise. No room was available, however; the convoy was full.

I started to cry. The sergeant looked at me, pointed to the ground and said, "Wait." He ran over to one of the drivers.

The trucks were packed completely full, the engines already running. As the convoy slowly started to move out, the sergeant came running back breathless but with a happy face, shouting over the roar of the engines, "Go! Hurry! They will make room."

The sergeant quickly pushed both of us onto a beige truck covered with a thick canvas roof, the children sitting inside in four long rows. The children cheered for us, several of them pulling us and our small canvas bags over the side. With their assistance, we climbed in, and squeezed tightly into the rear of the truck with the others.

PART SEVEN

Aliyah

I laughed and cried. The children were my age and younger — both boys and girls. The vibration of the truck and the wind blowing in our faces made us happy and we started to sing. Yiddish songs. Polish songs. Happy songs. Any happy song we could remember, we sang. We talked together, but not about the past. We only talked about the future. We planned our activities in our new home in Italy. We decided to create a singing group there, and even a theater group. Plans also developed for a soccer team. We decided we wanted to study Hebrew, and to learn about Palestine.

I enjoyed my seat in the rear of the truck because I could see out of the opening in the canvas cover. We passed the most beautiful mountainous scenery I had ever seen, finally descending into a valley on the Austrian side of the border with Italy, just past the city of Villach. By now it was late afternoon, and darkness had begun to fall.

All of a sudden the small convoy of army trucks left the highway, veered off onto a side road, and stopped completely. A Jewish Brigade motorcyclist who was escorting the convoy stopped near my truck, and a group of Jewish Brigade soldiers who seemed to appear from nowhere came over to talk to him. Our drivers and other escorts hopped out of their cabs and joined the brief discussion. These soldiers looked heroic in their uniforms and big floppy berets, but we wondered what was going on. I began to feel the tension.

A soldier left the group and came to talk to us. He looked very serious and said: "Listen to me very carefully. We are about to cross two border checkpoints. This is the most dangerous part of the journey because your presence must not be detected by anyone. We must smuggle you across the border into Italy. If the border guards find you, they will send you back."

This message scared me and the rest of the children more than anything else he could have said. We were terrified at the thought of returning to Austria, and would do anything to prevent it. He continued to talk. "We will cover the front and rear openings of the truck with canvas and will tie it closed with rope. You will not be able to see, but you will hear the truck stop at the checkpoints. When we stop, you should not make any sound — do not even breathe. I know this is frightening for you all, but after we cross the border we will reach our camp and you will be safe."

Sure enough, the soldiers covered the openings of our truck with canvas and tied the canvas closed as we sat huddled together like cargo on the benches. Once the truck was completely covered, the soldier's voices sounded muddled, and I felt as though we were in a submarine. Soon the truck started to move. I felt the vibration of the engine as the truck shifted gears and began to move faster. Picking up speed, we stayed on the highway for a little while but then, as the soldier had warned us, we came to a complete stop.

I held my breath. I could hear the doors of the truck cab open as our soldier and driver got out. I could hear them speaking in English and even joking around with the Americans. When I heard the laughter I felt more relaxed. But I still tried to hold my breath.

Soon we started moving again. Finally, we could breathe. But a few minutes later, the truck stopped again. This time there was no laughter. Our soldier and driver left the cab of the truck and came around to the back near where I was sitting. I could hear the soldiers talking to someone — it sounded like they were explaining what was in the back of the truck, but I could neither hear nor understand their words. A few seconds later the truck cab doors slammed and we began to move again.

I felt relieved. But I also realized that this "border check" was looser than usual. Obviously, it had been prearranged. We nevertheless were safe, and realizing it, we started to laugh. Soon afterwards our truck, as well as the others, stopped again, this time to remove the covers. We sang with relief.

We reached the Italian city of Tarvisio, a beautiful place in a small valley. The mountains and trees that surrounded the valley made me feel secure and protected. We entered a well-organized British army camp staffed by the Jewish Brigade and filled with many other Jewish children. We knew some of them from Salzburg, and felt happy to see them again. After registration, we were assigned to our beds. I was exhausted from the journey, and fell asleep.

In the morning we were awakened by a soldier who entered our army barrack blowing a military whistle. He said in Hebrew, *"Kulam lakum!,"* or "Everybody get up!" We quickly proceeded to a big army dining room, where we ate breakfast. Then we were asked to walk to a parade ground, where the soldiers were preparing to raise the Jewish flag. The flag had a white background and a blue Star of David in the middle. I had not seen the Jewish flag since my B'nai Akiva days. I watched while orders were given to the soldiers to raise the ropes that hoisted the flag. I was thrilled to see these Jewish soldiers from Palestine raising the Jewish flag in Italy.

I turned to Hershel, who stood next to me, and whispered, "I never thought I would see our flag again." I could see that he, too, was moved.

After the flag was raised, the base commander spoke to us.

"Welcome, children. You are now under the care of the Jewish Brigade from Palestine, the Land of Israel."

We all fell silent.

"You are in Tarvisio, Italy. From here we will travel together in a convoy until we get to a village called Santa Maria. This village is in southern Italy, a beautiful place."

We started to whisper among ourselves. I turned to Hershel and said: "Will we ever get to Palestine?"

"SHHHH," he said to me impatiently, "We will get there. Just listen."

"Children, quiet, please," the sergeant continued. "You will be on the shore of the Adriatic Sea. You will be able to swim there. You will be with many other children. You will have teachers so that you may study. You will be provided with clean laundry. You will also be provided with plenty of food. You can eat as much as you want. There is no need to store or to hide any."

When he said this, I looked down at the floor. I felt ashamed. We each had been hiding food after our meals and we were under an illusion that no one else knew about it. I felt like an animal when I did it, and I knew it was wrong, but I trusted no one. I felt a strong urge to protect myself by ensuring that I always had a supply of food. But it was embarassing when a small bit of bread fell out of my clothes or blanket. When this happened I looked around to make sure no one had seen.

The soldier continued. "You will have clean beds to sleep on. Showers every day. You can play soccer. There will also be entertainment for you. I hope that each of you will feel comfortable. Most important, you will be under the protection of representatives from the Jewish Agency in Palestine. You will be part of the Youth Aliyah program; we will prepare you for your new lives in Palestine. You will learn Hebrew, history, geography."

We were excited. We began to clap our hands, and we smiled.

"One more thing," the sergeant interrupted. "While you are on the journey to Santa Maria, you must obey our instructions. You may not leave the camp area. If you need anything, tell us, and we will try to help you. This is for your protection and safety." Then he added, "And later today we will provide each of you with a hot shower with soap. You do not have to push. Each of you will have a chance."

I had not had a hot shower with soap for a very long time. I did not even remember what a hot shower felt like. I could hardly wait until later.

After lunch two British army trailers with mobile field showers moved into the camp. Each trailer had five showers. We lined up and waited our turn. We sang and shoved each other playfully while we waited. When it was my turn, I received a piece of soap and ran happily into the shower. It was hot, and I tried to wash away Concentration Camp Ebensee from my soul. I could have stayed an hour, but my turn was soon over. I dried off and put on the clean, oversized army uniform the Jewish Brigade provided and walked like a new person to a discussion about Palestine.

That evening, Friday night, we had our first Sabbath dinner since the ghetto. We sat at long rectangular tables covered with white paper. A girl was chosen to light the Sabbath candles. We watched her recite the blessing, and then we all quietly said "Amen." As I watched her light the candles, I remembered that in the camps I had felt that I would probably never live to see the candles lit again on the Sabbath. I felt terribly sad, remembering my mother's face as she spoke to God on Friday evenings.

We were asked to rise for the *Kiddush*. One of the boys chanted the *Kiddush* in a voice that reminded me of a cantor's. We were in a trance as we watched and listened to him sing. The melody was beautiful, and I quickly realized that I had not forgotten the words.

The soldiers had obtained freshly-baked white bread for us. The bread looked a little like my mother's *challah*, and in my mind she was near me and had baked me a special *challah* roll. She handed me a glass of tea with honey. "Have a sweet life, my darling." I began to cry softly to myself, and then I realized that in my sadness I had missed the rest of the blessings.

Despite my sadness, the dinner that night was wonderful. We were served meat and potatoes, and there was enough for seconds and even more. We ate fruit for the first time in many years. I felt lucky and satisfied, but I was sad. I could not stop thinking about my family.

We sang songs — Yiddish ones that we remembered, and Hebrew ones that we were learning. One of the soldiers played an accordion, and, sensitive to our sadness, led us in singing only happy songs. We went to bed that night with full stomachs, and with faith and hope that we would maybe find someone in our families alive.

Next morning I awoke again to the sharp sound of a military whistle. A soldier stood at the entrance to our sleeping area. *"Kulam lakum!"* he shouted into the barrack. "Everybody get up!" I was in a good mood, excited to be on the way to Palestine. But I could have slept a lot longer. I turned to Hershel, who was lying next to me, already awake.

"Why are we moving out so early?" I said to him. "Is this another *Appel?"*

"Sort of," he grumbled, also tired. "Let's hurry to the toilets."

"We do not have to run to the toilets, Hershel. There is no rush. We are not in the camps," I reminded him. "But we have to get up. They are ready to read our names."

There were no more *Appels* in our life. But the soldiers still came into our sleeping quarters every morning to call out our names. They taught us to reply in Hebrew: *"Kan!,"* or "Here!"

I was anxious to leave this camp and arrive at our permanent destination, as were all the children. We were nervous that we would be discovered by the British army, which controlled parts of Italy, and that they would forbid us from continuing on our journey. The British did not want refugees travelling in their army trucks, as we were doing. They felt it was a "waste" of precious fuel and personnel to use trucks for civilian purposes.

After breakfast we boarded the trucks. I shared a truck with a group of 40 children. We sat on benches most of the time, but I liked to stand in the front so that I could enjoy the views of the mountains and, as we proceeded down the coast of Italy, the Adriatic Sea. I had never seen the sea before, and it excited me. I wished I could swim in the waves or ride a sailboat. Those activities seemed exotic.

Other children wanted to enjoy the view as well, and we fought over who would sit in the front or back, which were the preferred seats. Seats in the middle were less desirable because the canvas sides obstructed the view. I was lucky always to have a seat reserved for me in the front because the other children liked me to lead them in singing songs.

For lunch we stopped on the side of the road and ate the army food packages the Jewish Brigade soldiers had collected for us. We slept for a few nights in camps that had been arranged in advance. Our journey flew by as we sang songs and told jokes, played games and waved at the Italians we passed as we travelled.

A few days later we arrived in a United Nations Relief and Rehabilitation Agency, or UNRRA, refugee camp in the port of Bari, where some of the soldiers left our group. From there we continued further south to a fishing village at the southern tip of Italy, right on the Adriatic, called Santa Maria di Bagni. This was to be our final destination in Italy. We arrived in the afternoon.

As we jumped out of our trucks, the UNRRA camp Commandant greeted us. "Welcome to the UNRRA camp of Santa Maria di Bagni!" he said, smiling.

Then the Youth *Aliyah* representatives of the Jewish Agency ran over to us and introduced themselves.

We would be under their supervision, and they would prepare us for immigration to Palestine.

This was a beautiful place. It did not look at all like a refugee camp. There was no barbed wire, no gate, no guards. This was a resort town, and I could see people swimming in the sea. Originally requisitioned by the Allied authorities for Yugoslavian refugees, the houses where we were to live were former summer residences. They were two stories high, and each room faced the sea. We were surrounded by lush landscaping. Fig trees were planted in back of the houses. In another month we would be able to harvest the fruit.

We were told to line up for a medical examination. While we waited, older refugees ran up to us hoping to find people they knew. I saw a man I knew from Plaszow.

"How long have you been here? How do you like it here?"

"We are here only about a month," he replied. "We are part of a *kibbutz* group preparing to make *aliyah* to Palestine. We do not know how long we will have to stay, but it is nice here in Santa Maria. You will like it."

As I was listening, I was startled to hear my name. "Lazorek!"

I turned around, shocked to see Esther, my former housemate in the ghetto. Esther had saved my life by finding me work at the AFL base. She hugged and kissed me for a long time. I asked her if she had seen anyone from my family.

"No, Lazorek. I haven't seen anyone," she said sadly. "But I am so happy to see you."

"So who else have you seen since the liberation?" I asked.

"A few women from the AFL have survived. Fela, Edzia, Pola. I am not sure where they are now."

I had to go, but I promised to see her soon. I was taken into a room that served as a medical office, where an UNRRA medical officer asked me questions about my health. He checked my ears, my throat, and my eyes, and examined my head for lice. Though he found none, he sprinkled DDT on me just to be sure.

After the examination, we registered and were assigned to our rooms. My room was located on the second story, and it contained four beds and a chair or two, but no other furniture. Sitting on top of each bed were two blankets and a mess kit. I was assigned three roommates, Monyek, Judke and Tsvika. We selected our beds, and I was lucky to have the one next to the window, overlooking the sea.

Hershel was assigned to another room in my building. I felt sad that we would not share a room — he had been my friend for longer than anyone I knew. I felt disconnected. Our lives were about to expand beyond anything we had known. We were going to study, to form new relationships, to become healthy again and to reintegrate into society.

Two of my new roommates were from Lodz, Poland, and one from Lithuania. All had been in the camps. We quickly became friends. That evening we attended a meeting with the Youth *Aliyah* representatives. We were told that our group was to be called *Atid,* or "the future," that this would be our home until we embarked on our voyage to Palestine, and that we would study Hebrew and other subjects. We were introduced to our houseparents.

I liked this place. I enjoyed making new friends, sharing a room with only three boys, and being able to eat plenty of food. I gained a lot of weight. Soon a shipment arrived of supplemental household supplies that the American Joint Distribution Committee, or the "Joint," sent for the Youth *Aliyah* groups. Some of us received white sheets, towels, soap, toothbrushes and even toothpaste. With over 400 children in the village, there was not enough for all of us, but we shared as best we could. Sometimes the Joint sent us clothes as well. This was a welcome supplement to the oversized military uniforms we had been wearing.

We were divided into eight groups, and each group was given a Hebrew name: *Hatikvah* (the hope), *Geulim* (redeemed), *Gur Ariyeh* (young lions), *Atid* (future), *Moledet* (homeland), *Tzabarim* (native of the Land of Israel), *Dror* (liberty) and *Frumka. Frumka* was filled with girls; there were mostly boys in our group. We were proud to be given these Hebrew names. They symbolized our new-found freedom and strength.

I enjoyed having interesting things to do in a boarding school, or Youth Village, setting. I was resuming my studies. We studied Hebrew, Jewish history, general history, geography of Palestine, and agricultural subjects. The Joint sent some books and other school materials. But there were shortages of books, pencils, and paper. We shared with each other or learned orally.

We found other things to do to pass the time until we could go to Palestine. I joined a drama group that was headed by a friend named Monyek. We performed plays and sang for the entire Youth *Aliyah* village of Santa Maria. The Jewish Agency, with the help of the Jewish Brigade, found costumes and props for us to use. My favorite play was one we made up about a ship that sailed for the Land of Israel. We also performed old Yiddish songs that expressed our longing for our families and our former lives.

My favorite, "I Want To See My Home One More Time," had a beautiful melody, and words that expressed my feelings better than I could. "I want to see my home again. Is it the same as it was before? Here is the tree and here is the bench. Here is the roof that is falling apart. But this is still my little, sweet home."

We were kept busy, studying in makeshift classrooms and in the afternoons gathering for cultural activities. We heard enchanting stories from our Israeli houseparents about pioneers of the Zionist movement in the Land of Israel.

It was at night that the terror returned. I would awaken to the sounds of crying and screaming. Many children would relive their experiences in the camps, and it would haunt us all. Our houseparents would comfort us, but it was hard to fall back asleep.

I had nightmares often. I dreamed that I was being chased until I fell exhausted into a bottomless, dark tunnel. Falling uncontrollably, I would yell for my Mama, who would not appear. I would awaken from one of these nightmares sobbing. Monyek would turn on the light, the houseparents would come into the room and calm me down, but I could not sleep for hours afterwards, thinking about my mother. I missed her terribly.

Afternoons we had free time to swim in the sea or walk into the fishing village. One afternoon Hershel and I decided to walk, with some other friends, into a nearby village, Santa Croce, to see a movie. I had not been in a movie theater since my brother slipped me money to attend the Kino Apollo in Radom.

We left without telling the Jewish Brigade soldiers or anyone else, afraid they would not let us go. We walked for hours to a small movie theater in the center of Santa Croce. We saw a black and white Charlie Chaplin movie, "The Great Dictator." We understood not one word of the American film and could not read the vertical Italian subtitles, but we laughed and laughed the entire time. On the way back to Santa Maria, we lost our way, and did not arrive until dawn. The Jewish Brigade soldiers were angry with us for this adventure.

The aim of the entire operation in Italy was to prepare refugees for *aliyah,* or immigration to Palestine. Refugees came from all over Europe to Italy under the impression that ships were waiting to take them to Palestine. As the Chairman of the Refugee Committee in

Santa Maria said to a member of the Allied Commission who had arrived on a visit: "We ask from you only one thing — *aliyah*; we wish to hear from you only one thing — *aliyah*; we have only one will and one hope — *aliyah*."

It soon became clear that serious and tragic shortages of immigration certificates were hampering these efforts. The British government was restricting the very *aliyah* that was the only hope of Hitler's victims. Bitterness and disappointment pervaded the refugee camps as weeks turned to months and few certificates were issued.

Even immigration of children was restricted. We waited for six months with little word about when, how many, and which of us would be allocated the precious and rare immigration certificates. The Jewish Agency Immigration Department found itself faced with making decisions as to how to handle immigration requests from the many thousands of orphaned children, as well as those of children whose parents were sick or who simply wanted their children to be free of the refugee camps.

The Youth *Aliyah* program was reserved primarily for orphaned children between the ages of 15 and 17. Children with parents still alive were permitted to join the program, but only if their parents were too ill to care for them. Younger children were considered inappropriate for the program because of the increased responsibility of taking care of them. The Youth *Aliyah* program decided how many certificates for its children should be requested from the Jewish Agency Immigration Department. Then the Immigration Department made the contacts with the British government to secure the limited number of visas and arranged the transportation.

My group, *Atid,* was finally notified it was our turn to receive certificates. We could not contain our joy. We clapped our hands, screamed, and jumped up in the air. We found out later that one of the other groups in my village had been denied certificates, and would not be joining us. Like many, this group would be delayed by the shortage of available immigration certificates.

On October 30, 1945, Hershel and I left Santa Maria on Jewish Brigade trucks for Bari, where we spent four days in the UNRRA refugee camp. There, we filled out the required paperwork and were photographed for the immigration officials. Finally, the day arrived for us to leave Europe.

ॐ

Early in the morning on November 4, 1945, we boarded the Jewish Brigade trucks for the last time. I had never been on a ship before, and I could not wait to be on board. Yet I was a little scared. As a child I had seen pirate movies at the Kino Apollo in Radom. I was afraid of travelling through a storm and being attacked by pirates.

Our trucks travelled to Taranto harbor, Italy, where we picked up our immigration certificates. The next day, we saw our ship, a converted supply ship, the "Princess Kathleen." It looked huge. We said goodbye to the Jewish Brigade soldiers and to the Youth *Aliyah* representatives who were there to help organize our boarding. We stood in line with refugees outside our group — pregnant women and other adults, also boarding. The British soldiers checked each certificate carefully.

With my friends, I boarded. It was 1:30 p.m., November 5, 1945. I wanted to remember this important date, so I wrote it down in a little black book that I carried. The ship started to move, and I felt a wonderful sensation. I was on the way to freedom in the Land of Israel.

I wished more than anything that my family could be there. I could see my mother before my eyes, uttering her final words to me. "If there is anyone in the family with a chance to survive, it is you. Have a sweet life."

We slept in hammocks for the four-day voyage from the Gulf of Taranto and into the Mediterranean Sea. The weather was stormy for two days, and we were all seasick. Hershel was sicker than all the rest, and I tried to help him. When the storms subsided, I stood for a long time on the upper deck and enjoyed the sea breeze blowing into my face. On the day before we were due to arrive, Monyek and I organized our drama group to perform a show, "A Journey Around the World." All of us were emigrants from different places in Europe, and we had a lot to share about our prior lives. The passengers and the crew came to hear us singing songs from many different countries. We sang for hours, and everyone enjoyed the show.

Early the next morning, the captain announced over the loudspeakers that we were approaching Haifa harbor. Hershel and I raced up to the deck in competition to be the first to see land. We soon saw on the horizon a shadow that turned out to be the port.

We all saw the port at the same time. "I see it! I can see it!" I yelled.

"Me, too! I can't wait to get off the ship!" Hershel yelled back.

"But how much longer before we reach land?" I asked.

Hershel asked a crew member.

"Less than an hour more," he reported excitedly.

The last hour we stood on the deck, watching the land come closer. We saw that Haifa was a city built partly on a mountain, that there were warships in the harbor and white houses on the slopes. It looked beautiful.

The ship's engines went silent and the crew lowered the anchor. We disembarked onto smaller boats that were waiting to carry us ashore. Approaching the shore, we sang the *"Hatikvah,"* the Jewish anthem, and we held high the Jewish flag we had brought from Italy. We felt free at last.

ঽ৶

After we passed through the British Mandatory Authority checkpoint, the Jewish Agency Immigration Department boarded my group onto a bus, and we headed down the coast. We were told we would make a temporary stop for a few days, prior to entering our youth villages, for quarantine and disinfection. This was necessary to comply with the British Mandatory Authority health rules. We were escorted to our temporary facility by British soldiers in army vehicles.

I was unprepared for what I saw. As we drove up to the Atlit Detention Camp, I saw rows of long wooden barracks, surrounded by barbed wire and manned watchtowers. What I saw evoked images, which I had been trying to forget, of the Nazi concentration camps. It was apparent that thousands of refugees were living there, not on a temporary basis, but permanently. We found out later that these refugees had been caught by the British entering Palestine without certificates.

We did not want to enter this place, and we told the Jewish Agency representatives that we had not come to the Land of Israel to enter another concentration camp, even for a day. They reassured us that it would be temporary, that we would remain under their care and supervision, and that our studies and classes would continue.

Reluctantly we entered through the main gate, guarded by armed soldiers. When the gates were closed and locked, I felt for the first time since liberation that I was sealed in again — trapped. Everywhere I looked I could see barracks, barbed wire, and manned watchtowers. There was no direction I could look that was free from these Nazi symbols.

We registered with the British camp authorities,

and were told to proceed to disinfection barracks. We arrived at a large building, where a British soldier separated the boys from the girls. We showered, were sprayed with disinfectant, and redressed. From there we proceeded to our barracks.

We were disappointed. The barbed wire and guard towers were bad enough. But the forced disinfection and separation of boys from girls was the last straw. We were not afraid of them — we knew they were not Nazis, and we knew we were protected. So we decided to create some disorganization.

The next morning we were called out to a roll call in a central square. When the British asked us to stand in line to be counted, we refused, and instead walked back to the barracks. The Jewish Agency intervened, and arranged to have the British call our names in our barracks instead.

The Jewish Agency representatives were not happy with our attitude. They needed to encourage the co-operation of the British, and our behavior angered them. Especially the next morning, after we developed a plan.

We took a bucket filled with water, and placed it on top of a board over the door to our barracks. We waited next to our beds. When the British corporal pushed the door open, the bucket turned over and all of the water spilled on him. The Jewish Agency worker who was following him got wet as well. We all laughed while the corporal cursed us.

His threat of punishment curbed any further

rebellious activities until our departure from Atlit four days later. We felt better after that. We ignored the barbed wire as we studied and prepared to go on to our boarding schools.

One day Hershel was called to the camp office. A man had seen his name in a newspaper notice of our group's arrival and was there to see if Hershel was one of his relatives. The man was waiting outside the barbed wire fence. Hershel ran to the fence and saw a nice-looking man dressed in a business suit. They realized that the man was indeed Hershel's uncle, and he told Hershel he would make arrangements to take him.

Hershel was thrilled. He had never seen this uncle before, but he would be with his family. He could work with his uncle in the diamond business. Hershel counted the days until the uncle would return to take him to Tel Aviv.

I was jealous. I wished that I also would get a visit from a relative. I knew that I had some family in Tel Aviv, but I did not know where. Every time a message came, I hoped it was for me.

The day arrived for Hershel to leave. I walked him to the camp gate. We hugged each other tightly.

"I will keep in touch with you, Lyzerke," he promised. "I know how to find you. And you have my address."

"You must come to visit me in my new school. And I will come to see you in Tel Aviv," I replied.

We remained in Atlit for seven days, during which

time Youth *Aliyah* workers asked us whether we wanted a religious or a secular education. I chose a secular education, as did the majority of my *Atid* group. We were then assigned to the Mossad Magdiel Agricultural School, located in the Sharon Valley. On November 14, 1945, finally released from the Atlit Detention Camp, we were taken by bus to Magdiel.

౫

Magdiel was my first home since I had left Radom. At first I felt happy with my old friends, and made new friends from among the Israeli children in the school. The teachers were kind to us, helping us integrate into society. We were provided with medical, psychological, and dental treatment if we needed it. We were given new clothing and shoes. Our studies continued. I saw Hershel occasionally.

But Magdiel was not near a city — it was isolated — and I began to get bored. There were too many rules and regulations. We had to be in class at certain times, to bed at certain times. We could not leave Magdiel without telling someone where we were going. I didn't like to live under anyone's control.

I decided to run away to a nearby religious youth village, which I had heard was less restrictive than Magdiel. It turned out that a religious education was not what I wanted either, so I decided to leave there as well. I wanted more than anything to see if I had any family still alive.

I remembered that my mother had a brother in Tel Aviv who had helped us when we were trying to emigrate to Palestine before the war. I knew his last name, but not his first. I went directly to the office of the Radom Association in Tel Aviv. They knew my uncle and sent someone to take me to his home.

When I arrived, my uncle cried.

"You know I tried to help your parents get a visa," he said, wiping his eyes. "But it did not work out. Do you know if anyone else from our family survived?"

"I am afraid not. At least I don't know of anyone so far," I replied, crying.

He hugged me tightly. "You must stay here with us tonight. Do you plan to leave your school?"

Before I could answer, my cousins, having been alerted of my arrival by the man from the Radom Society, started to stream into my uncle's house. They wanted to see what a Holocaust survivor looked like, to hear stories about the Holocaust.

They wanted to know how I had managed to survive. My uncle intervened. "Don't ask him all your questions right now. He must be tired. Ask him later."

I was relieved. I did not want to talk to my cousins about my survival. They left, and I went to bed.

The next day my cousin Ya'acov came to discuss with me my future plans. He suggested that I stay in Tel Aviv; he would help me learn a profession and find a job. I decided to try to work, and not to return to the youth village.

The next two and a half months I worked in the construction trade. Except for my visits with Hershel, who was living nearby, I was unhappy and bored. I did not know Hebrew, so I could not communicate, I could not understand radio shows or news, and I could not read the newspaper. I felt disconnected.

Hershel, who had by now changed his name to the Hebrew name "Tzvi," had happy news. He had found his sister in America. She had made arrangements for him to go to her. We said goodbye, and, although he promised to visit, I knew I would not see him for a long time. Tzvi's leaving upset me. I was happy for him, but I felt alone again. He had been my only link to my past.

But for my cousin Yaffa, I had no other friends. I did not have anything in common with the teenagers in my neighborhood in Tel Aviv. They were religious for the most part, and I felt the religious life too restrictive. I wanted to learn during the day and dance at night. I did not want to sit home.

I was invited to share dinner at my distant cousins' homes every Friday night for weeks. As the only survivor from the family, they all wanted to meet me and to find out how a survivor looked. They asked me many questions about the camps and the ghettos, but I felt that they did not approve of my answers.

They felt that we had not fought for our lives, that we had allowed the Germans to destroy Polish Jewry. They did not understand the circumstances facing the Jews in Poland before and during the war, and information about organized and spontaneous Jewish resistance in Poland and elsewhere had not been revealed.

I became upset and ashamed. I could not explain what had happened, and confronted by subtle accusations that we victims were responsible for our own fate, I began to believe they were right. I began to feel guilty about surviving. I determined to avoid further discussion about the subject of the Holocaust. I decided to erase it from my past and to hide my identity as a survivor.

One of my cousins, a teacher named Shoshana, sensed that I needed to return to school with my friends from Italy, that I needed to establish my identity in an atmosphere free from guilt. She convinced me to return to the Youth *Aliyah* program. But the Jewish Agency was frustrated with me because I had left the program. They did not believe that I would stay this time.

But they gave me another chance. I had convinced them that I wanted to go to Jerusalem. It had been my family's dream, and I wanted to realize that dream. There was an opening at an agricultural school named Chavat Halimud. Some of the students there had been with me in Italy, but there were native-born students as well.

I arrived at my new school in Jerusalem on March 11, 1946. I knew right away that this place was for me. The students were happy. The teachers and native-born students did not pressure us to talk about our suffering in the camps and the loss of our families. The studies were interesting. I could work in the flower gardens in the afternoon and take a bus into the center of the city any time I wanted. Rules were relaxed and the professionals were flexible. I was free.

※

The sign that this was the right place for me stood in one corner of the grounds. Big white boxes contained beehives. A man with a net over his face cultivated the hives. Every day I would be able to eat honey. I had not seen honey since my mother had given me that cup so many years ago. When I first saw the beehives, I felt I was receiving a message from my mother that I would find happiness here — that I would have a sweet life. *"Beshert."*

Epilogue

A sealed room in Jerusalem. January, 1991. The clearance siren sounds. The threat is over, at least for now.

I had passed out, but I am awake now. My wife brings me a cup of tea. She and my daughter do not understand why I act so strangely. Slowly, emotionally, I begin to explain to them my feelings about the gas — that I feel the need to protect them from it as I was not able to do for my family almost 50 years ago. I cannot bear to feel so helpless again. To be a victim.

All of a sudden I need them to know what happened to me — to understand my shame and guilt. After 47 years I must tell them the story. I must unlock the door of the "sealed room" that was my childhood. The story must be released from deep inside my soul. The story must release me — to relieve the great burden I have carried. This was how it happened....

A Special Note from Eli

I searched for my family for many years after the war. I thought there was a chance that someone from my family — maybe my brother Abush Hershenfis, who was daring and athletic — might have jumped off the train and escaped Treblinka. But I haven't found a trace of him, or of any other member of my family.

I married a girl I met in the Chavat Halimud Agricultural School, Rivka Winer, and developed a career as a tour guide in Israel. This made it possible for me to share my deep love for the Land of Israel, which was imbued within me by my parents since early childhood. For more than 20 years I worked with missions from the United Jewish Appeal, the fund-raising organization in America connected with the Jewish Agency for Israel, which was responsible for bringing me to the shores of the Land of Israel in November 1945.

I also took a Hebrew surname, "Ayalon," a beautiful valley in central Israel that is mentioned in the Bible, and a Hebrew version of my first name, "Eliezer." People call me by the nickname "Eli." I fought in the War of Independence in 1948, and later became a soldier in the Israel Defense Forces.

But for most of those years, I hid from everyone that I came from Poland and that I am a Holocaust survivor. I did not tell my story to anyone because I felt guilty that I was the only member of my family to survive, and I felt that I must have done something wrong in order to do so. There was a perception in society at the time that the victims of the Holocaust must have done something to deserve it. Many people did not realize then what society has finally recognized — that the Jews of Europe were defenseless and helpless during the Second World War.

In a chance meeting in the 1980s, I had a discussion with Elie Wiesel, the famous Holocaust author, historian, and teacher. I told him that I had not been able to tell my story. He said that it was my obligation to speak out and to tell the world about the Holocaust. He told me that I had survived for a reason — to tell the world what had happened to my family and to me.

Suddenly, I remembered that my mother had once told me the same thing — that it was *beshert* that I survive to tell the story of my family. Then, in December, 1991, on a United Jewish Appeal mission group from Baltimore, I met my author, Neile Friedman, and her husband, John. Neile had studied the Holocaust for many years, and had professional experience, as a lawyer, in eliciting information from reluctant witnesses. Using these skills, as well as a natural curiosity, Neile was able to draw out from me this story. What is most remarkable is how she was able to help me recreate the details — the colors, smells, names, and shapes of my past — and all that after having buried the memories for 47 years. The honey simply flowed from the cup!

I have been back to my home in Radom three times. On my first visit in 1990, with my wife, I attempted to get inside my home on Vitolda Street. The apartment is now an umbrella repair shop. The Polish tenant, however, would not allow us to enter the shop, for fear that we would try to reclaim it.

On my third visit to Poland, in 1994, I again took my wife, Rivka, along with our son, Ofer and grandson, Gil. Gil is now a Lieutenant in the IDF. He was deeply affected by his personal encounter with the tragic events of my lost childhood. Gil pointed out to me how ironic it is that he is responsible for defending the borders of Israel, in contrast to the defenselessness of his grandfather more than 50 years ago.

Since Gil's trip to Poland, my other grandchildren have also connected with the past. Gil's sister, Yifat (now a Corporal and training commander in the IDF), along with her high school class, visited the extermination site at Treblinka where her forbearers perished. Yifat and Gil's younger sister, Neta, as well as my daughter Nurit's son, Omri, are now learning about the Holocaust in elementary school, and are writing poems and stories about their grandfather's family and childhood to share with their class. My youngest grandson, Almog, whose mother was pregnant with him during the Gulf War, will also learn about his grandfather's past — perhaps by reading a Hebrew translation of this book.

To help me tell the story, Neile and I took a trip to Radom and to the other places of my childhood in 1993. This was my second visit to Radom. We walked the cobblestones that have not been replaced in 50 years. We stood at the corner of Shvarlikovska Street where I last saw my mother and my sister. We visited the square where my family was forced to stand for their selection during their deportation to Treblinka. Near the former Rychul Market we saw the Kino Apollo movie house. On Valova Street we saw the recently-erected monument on the site of the large synagogue, which was destroyed during the war.

On this visit, the tenant who lived in my former home was friendlier, perhaps because his wife was about to make a trip to America, and I was accompanied by an American. My home looked the same as it had 50 years earlier — the floor tiles had not even been replaced in the hallway leading to the basement. The courtyard where we used to play soccer was there, as were the windows to the former "Zalman's Restaurant." To my great dismay, however, the tenant of my home had recently replaced the original stove, or *piecyk,* on which my mother had cooked all our meals. More than anything in my home, the stove was a symbol of my lost family, and I was sad that it was no longer there.

We took a tour of the former AFL base, which was used during the war as an army supply depot, and which is still in use today — as a tobacco factory. This building, like many buildings in Radom, has not been renovated in 50 years. The low ceilings of the former storage rooms are still supported by the original heavy columns, and the wooden railroad ramp (where I had fallen and broken my leg) still stood outside the heavy wooden doors.

In Austria we visited the Mauthausen concentration camp and the site of the Melk camp. We stood on the platform where I had waited for the trains to take me to work in the underground tunnels. We wanted to visit the tunnels as well, but they had recently been closed for cleaning because of vandalism. We then drove on the road, along the Danube River, where I was forced to march from Melk to Ebensee during that terrible spring of 1945.

We also wanted to see the former Plaszow camp, near Kraków, Poland, but because the camp was destroyed after the war, we felt that the visit would be futile. But, several months before our trip, we happened to see an article in the *Jerusalem Post* that mentioned film director Steven Spielberg was building a replica of the Plaszow camp for the film "Schindler's List." After writing to Spielberg, we received an invitation from the film's producer, Jerry Molen, to visit the set.

On March 31 and April 1, 1993, Neile and I visited the movie set as guests. We watched filming, walked through the authentic-looking replica of the Plaszow Camp, and ate meals with the crew. We sat with the actors as they socialized or rehearsed their lines while drinking coffee and eating sweet cakes or thick soup in a small, privately owned coffeehouse, named "Ariel," on the grounds of the set. Seeing the "helpless" Jews and the SS officers barking orders, I was transported back to 1944, and recalled the nightmare of the Holocaust. I also shared some of my first-hand knowledge of the behavior of the camp's former Commandant, Amon Goeth, with the actor who portrayed him, Ralph Fiennes. During the experience on this set, I was touched by the unusual spirit and sense of mission shared by the film's producers, actors, and staff.

Today, I am finally able to include stories about my past in my guiding. And I lecture at Yad Vashem (Israel's memorial to the Jewish Holocaust victims), and at schools, universities, and conferences, in the United States and in Israel. I now am eager to tell my story, and I no longer feel the need to hide my identity as a survivor.

Spilling my cup of honey has once again brought to life the memory of my lost family. The most valuable aspect of telling my story is to perpetuate the memory of my dear family, among the millions of Jewish victims of the Holocaust. I also hope that, by reading my story as well as others like it, the next generation will learn the lessons of the Holocaust — that hate and intolerance were defeated by hope and courage.

I would like to extend my special thanks and appreciation to my author, Neile Sue Friedman, for her outstanding perseverance, patience, and devotion to this project. She spent hundreds of hours researching, inter-viewing, and writing and rewriting this book. Thanks to her, I was able to face my past and to talk about it. I hope that my story, and the stories of others like me, will further the teaching and understanding of the Holocaust. Neile played an essential role in bringing my part of this history to light.

I would also like to thank Neile's husband, John, whose dedication to his wife and to this project made possible the completion of this book. John not only created and masterminded the technical aspects of the project; on many occasions, he tirelessly and patiently assumed family duties so Neile could devote her attention to writing.

I must also mention their lovable children, Lily, Anna, and Joseph, who understood the importance of the project, and who proudly shared with their teachers and schoolmates at Krieger Schechter Day School their family's involvement in the project. They supported the venture with enthusiasm, even though their mother was at the computer for many hours that she would otherwise have spent playing with them, and I am very grateful for that.

A special thanks goes to Neile's parents, Jacqueline and Robert Smelkinson, for their unwavering guidance and support. I also appreciate their technical and creative assistance, which was instrumental to publication of this book. Finally, I owe a debt of gratitude to my dear, beloved wife, Rivka. Her inspiration and wisdom gave me the courage to begin and complete this project. My children and grandchildren gave strength and hope, which helped me uncover the past.